MY LUNCH WITH
A HOLLYWOOD
AGENT

MY LUNCH WITH A HOLLYWOOD AGENT

... what's on the menu?
... check back cover ...

By
Barry Leonardini

REGENT PRESS
Berkeley, California
2020

Table of Contents

Chapter I
Retrospective and Future

I am on my way to meet an old friend for lunch at Alioto's on San Francisco's Fisherman's Wharf. His name is Bernie Glow. Now in his late seventies, he still is a top Hollywood agent. It's the best business in Hollywood. Stars may come and go, producers and directors have fallouts with studios and backers, union troubles, salary disputes. But agents endure. Bernie was born in nineteen forty-three. His eventual profession was roughly laid out before him in nineteen forty-eight. Although he didn't become aware of the profession or the details till much much later.

In nineteen forty-eight Paramount Pictures made a settlement of an antitrust case with the United States Justice Department. All other studios became bound to it's terms also. It was called the Hollywood Antitrust Case of 1948. It changed the business model of Hollywood makers of motion pictures. It radically changed production, distribution and exhibition of films. Simply, studios could no longer be guaranteed that their films would be shown in a timely fashion or in desirable locales. That is because the Settlement stopped the studios from also owning theaters themselves. A great degree of risk was now added into choosing and casting and making of a film because of that settlement. As it turned out, that decision greatly expanded the potential of Bernie life's profession as an agent. He didn't know it at the time. He was five years old.

William Shakespeare together with his repertory owned the Globe Theater. It was a collaboration. Collaboration and spontaneity are a very important components for making believable quality entertainment. They were all in it together. How many of Shakespeare's plays were enhanced by individual members of the repertory contributing a word here or a gesture there? They also were comforted by the fact they knew they would have a close by venue for their plays. Arguably Shakespeare and company would not have been as prolific or as successful if they didn't have certainty their work would be performed at a convenient venue. How many playwrights and screenwriters were born after nineteen forty-eight and never had their talent come to fruition ? As it ultimately turned out, technology opened the door for those screenwriters. One example in the extreme was Netflix. It went from delivering films to making their own films with their own production company. Remarkable.

Technology's transformative ability is a recurring event. For better or for worse. Companies like Microsoft and Apple give platforms to any one's ideas and creative ability.

Like Charles Dickens opening sentence in Tale of Two Cities, "It was the best of times/it was the worst of times/it was the age of wisdom/it was the age of foolishness/ it was the epoch of incredulity/ it was the season of light/ it was the season of darkness/ it was the spring of hope/ it was the winter of despair".

Charles Dickens words could overlay how technology has made humans less human. People's jobs replaced by silicon chips. Consequently the workers have to reinvent themselves to be more chip-like in some areas and less human to compete in the work place.

Technology patterns and platforms can project some ones talent into almost a cartoon. Transformative effects to the economies and culture travel as fast as the new gadget can be embedded. And then the transformer becomes transformed and effects others down the line differently. Differences among people come out and are indisputably outlined in a caricature depiction. New benchmarks of great wealth are compared to lack of wealth amongst the relativity untransformed parts of society. And what are both missing? What's the goal? More money and power? At what cost ? Loss of feeling for the natural world ?

There is one fact about rearranging the original

metaphysic with technology to suit real time greed—there will be a bill. In the end the human will have to recreate what it thought it could do without.

Along with the changes, comes envy by some who feel left out. Also come feelings of estrangement by the newly wealthy for heretofore a comfortable and an adequate living philosophy and habits. With great wealth nothing has to be endured. Despite the adequacies of the old and familiar. Discipline got them to success. Now they somewhat discard discipline. So it begins. Great joy and then the let down of making a new personal life to reflect that wealth. Things have turned the familiar on it's head. All of a sudden there isn't enough time in a twenty-four hour day. This was supposed to be fun. So how come some have to work harder for a goal that they had already achieved. Sounds like transformative has to be parsed for net benefit or deficit.

Agents like Bernie carry on unruffled because of his personal contacts. He didn't use Microsoft or Apple Apps. He didn't lose his place by relying on a tool that some one else could use just as well or better. He kept it personal. That's the best way to control ones destiny. And the bonus is one is still intact. Let the world move over. It's a heady feeling.

What about Paramount Pictures and the Department Of Justice? Shakespeare's writing is timeless. Here is an apropos example. It's from Henry VI: "The first thing we must do is kill all the lawyers".

Lawyers live and thrive on taking cheap shots at someone else's success. Truly, attorneys are parasites.

I suspect Charles Dickens would have agreed also.

The publics negative opinions of attorneys has remained constant and will grow until the lawyers stop being embedded in our personal lives with each new piece of government legislation.

Paramount decided to put itself up sale because of the change in its business model. The conglomerate Gulf And Western with the help of Wall Street financial counterfeiters bought Paramount Pictures in nineteen sixty-six. Roughly since then, motion pictures without a repertory studio system lost a great number of secondary and tertiary supporting actors. It lost the seasoning and nuance. Movies suffered from that loss of depth. Studio system actors and script writers churned movies out like a conveyor belt at a factory. Of course it didn't go unnoticed that scripts were mostly the same. But doing your craft whatever it may be has to improve your skill. From five movies a year to one movie every two years will certainly be noticed by the audience who are seeking to be teased by nuance. So the new paradigm of movie making compensated with gimmicks or special effects or louder presentation or speed of light images that has the false impression of worthwhile entertainment. Many new movies are starkly formulaic and thin on emotional content. The movie maker treats the new audiences as half human and half silicon chip creation. Audiences remember emotional experiences. They tend to forget light shows and Dolby sound tracks that shake the theaters. If the occasional epic film was successful then there would be sequels. Paramount made the Godfather trilogy when part of the G&W conglomerate. Godfather 1 and II worked. Godfather III didn't. Some how the gooey ham fisted word "conglomerate"doesn't belong in the motion picture business.

Natural evolution takes time. The universe is about thirteen point eight hundred billion years old. Our solar system is approximately four and one half billion years old. Our own planet earth is the same age. Rocks have been found in Northwestern Canada that are a little over four billion years old. We as a species have been around for approximately sixty thousand years. We are a sport on the evolutionary tree. As far as we can tell there has not been anything like us before. Our main defining trait is we are never satisfied. That trait flows from the physical fact that we have a more developed brain then other entities on the planet. With that "advantage"we do many things because we can not because we should. I reckon that fully ninety percent of our brains "inventions"should have been rejected and the time better spent taking a walk in the park. Our brains main inventions are fiat money and presumptuous laws. Money is our magic wand. Presumptuous laws are our self described authority to spend that same monopoly money on limitless endeavors. Those endeavors rely on our four billion year old planet to redeem in natural resources. Needless to say, we can create money faster than nature can redeem the buy order. We are a cartoon of acquisitive traits. "Enough"is a word that could become obsolete. Or there could be an "Enough"button on our computer. It still is our life to live. But enough relates to discipline. And that's our shortfall. I fear the planet will run out of natural resources faster than we will learn discipline. Homo sapiens? No. Rather homo frivolous.

One example of fiat money multiplied by presumptuous laws and multiplied again by lack of discipline which in total equals chaos is— — — Hollywood. And it applies to some gay moguls who operate there. I believe that there is a project afoot by them to gene edit the human genome for money and more political power. My reasoning and significant amount of real and circumstantial evidence will come later in the book. This is not a shoot from the hip plan by Hollywood. They want to improve the human genome as per their values. And make a significant amount of money while they are at it. And more power will come with the cash. Queer plan? Indeed. I looked up the word queer. There was one definition that had queer meaning "perverse or oblique"from a German word circa sixteenth century. The word queer predated Hollywood and it's gays.

Queer could be used to describe many human endeavors. Queer is contagious. If queer antics are done at the top of society then it will be broadcast throughout the rest of society at a faster rate. Monkey see. Monkey do. Our Pentagon has been doing queer projects since it was assembled. An example is the multiple atmospheric testing of thermonuclear explosions long after World War II. The South Pacific island of Bikini was disintegrated or vaporized along with hapless fish and reefs and whales. I referred to the Hollywood intent of improving the human genome. But I immediately disclaim it will be an improvement. I'm old fashioned.

In the past ten to twenty years Hollywood has been producing films which in retrospect serve as trailers for this Hollywood queer upcoming cultural and scientific venture. I still don't know whether they started out twenty years ago with a plan to gene edit the human or they just backed into it? I kind of favor the latter—they backed into it. My reason? It became apparent to the movie producers gay and otherwise that audiences could be taught almost any philosophy/ reality or lack of philosophy/reality if the screen was big enough and the sound loud enough to discourage quiet reflection. So money is fine. But why not add political power to the increase of money flows by tinkering and patenting human genome alterations and things will be almost too good to be true. It would be like one of the movies the gay moguls produce! Ironic.

I have no particular aversion to gays. I accept homosexuality as a fact. It has been around as long as recorded history. I have dealt with gays and lesbians and the rest of the LGBTQ+ acronym most of my adult life. Both in friendships, business and in the sport of fencing. I and they respect discipline and courtesy. But I question some of their goals and tactics that are being put forward by a loosely to a rigidly organized gay steering committee located largely in Hollywood.

I queried Wikipedia about the LGBTQ+ acronym and I found out that according to Wikipedia there are four genders. The four were enumerated but the total added up to twelve. Queer math? The twelve which includes the four were: "...Male, female, transgender, gender neutral, non-binary, agender, pan gender, genderqueer, two spirit, third gender, and all or none, or a combination of these."

In the interest of clarity the Hollywood steering committee should publish an official accounting of the correct number and their official names and what is the difference that are in the LGBTQ+ acronym. I'm confused. I believe most are confused about the acronym LGBTQ+ identity and their intentions. That includes members themselves that proclaim an initial in the acronym best describes themselves. But most are afraid to ask because the Supreme Court just stamped their approval on the whole group. Wise decision by Supreme Court? It's not an academic question. There are significant health issues that follow the gay life style. HIV/AIDS is one issue which is accompanied by many collateral social and medical maladies.

I submit, as a quasi "amicus curiae"—friend of the court—-that there are only three constructive genders. They are male and female and bisexual. The eight plus additional initials in the acronym are only a parsing of bisexuality. Leave the eight for private discussions for people who care. The LGBTQ+ rainbow banner is like a Hollywood produced light show. Powerful projections of the acronym on the public conscious serves to distort the comparatively meager and questionable initials of the LGBTQ+ acronym. That's basic Hollywood glitz.

All things considered, it would seem that the gays relatively short period of time being out of the closet, so to speak,has them trying to make up for lost time by aggressive merchandising of their brand. They are entitled to state their priorities and defend their rights. I resent the drip, drip, drip of propaganda and political correctness concerning some issues and affirmative action. It gets so old. More child -like center of attention quest than adult conversation. They have targeted school children for instructions in the gay life style. That's not queer. That's evil. We all have opinions. No matter what the Supreme Court rules.

According to the Gallup Poll the United States population has approximately four and one half percent of gays. Does Gallop breakdown the component initials of those responding in the positive? Gallup started polling gay numbers in two thousand and twelve. Since that date gays answering in the positive to the Gallup poll have increased roughly thirty percent. That's a faster growth rate than any other group or race or religion in the country. Looks like Hollywood's push of the LGBTQ+ brand is successful. Any other explanation? Other sign posts of gay progress and influence is the mention by the media of public figures if they are from team gay. Putting gay political progress in context, the age of the universe is approximately thirteen point eight billion years old. But since 2015, gay marriage has become the law of the land and in 2016 President Obama issued an executive order allowing transgenders the right to choose which bathroom or locker room to use. Regardless of what their birth certificate indicated their birth date sex was. Question. How did the universe get along without Hollywood's guidance and political clout? The executive order by President Obama also allowed transgenders to compete as a female in spite of the physical fact that the person was a fully formed male. What about thirteen plus billion years of time tested evolution? The consequences to the normal female in those sport competitions are predictably disastrous for women. These are headline examples. The quieter under the radar changes that gays push for include teaching grammar school aged children about the gay lifestyle option. Non sexual teachings by Socrates got the philosopher killed on charges of corruption of the youth. What subject matter is omitted today in grammar school to make way for instructing homosexual protocols? It's a life style that carries a risk of disease. It's not a popular life style. If it was, Pete Seeger or Bob Dylan would have written and sang about it.

Safe to say gay catch-up has been very successful in steering the culture in a direction that no one
had ever thought possible or advisable. It's also safe
to say that the Hollywood gays have gone too far too
fast. It's also safe to say that Al Jolson in black face is
more believable on any topic than affirmative action
President Barack Obama. But the steering committee
of the gay juggernaut comes out of Hollywood. That
puts an entirely different class of gay in power for
culture changing the country. They have money and
influence. And they will not be denied. More like a
screaming juvenile wanting attention.

In my view an example of a gay Hollywood mogul
with political clout that could be interested in funding a gene editing project would be some one like a
Dave Geffen type of individual. He for me personifies
modern day Hollywood people. It's pure speculation. I
have not heard anything to support my opinion. Gene
editing could be the next big thing that homo frivolous would want a share of. This is not a gay issue. But
gays have the power and the money to steer initial
applications of this god-like power in directions that
are questionable to say the least. In other words—
gay or not gay—- most investors would love to dive
in and be part of first round investing in gene editing.
But the super ego of a guy like Gaffen fits. One example of a cavalier, callous super ego is the fact that
Geffen Records published music by mass murderer
Charles Manson. Manson's song "Look At Your Game,
Girl" was recorded by Axl Rose and his group Gun's

N' Roses in 1993. It was a track on Gaffe Records produced album "The Spaghetti Incident". The title could
be a crude oblique reference to Manson and his cults
murdering of nine people in Los Angeles in 1969.
Which is now known as the Tate/LaBianca murders.
Some of the murdered were Italian and the homi-
cide took place at the Italian heritage name LaBianca
home.

If Geffen was a hood ornament, he would be
front and center on a restored Duesenberg posing
as an ostentatious statue of Apollo from B.C.E. Thats
the glitzy power he projects. The Duesenberg is also
probably speeding.

Queer is certainly appropriate when talking
about changing sexes via rearranging billion year old
genomes. I suspect when one lives long enough in
the Hollywood bubble any thing seems possible.

Legislation that gays have helped pass have
already the effect that they physically seek without an
operation or gene editing. But there's no money in
this reality. They need a patented procedure to sell.
Title VII of The Civil Rights Act Of 1964 allows for a
legal sex orientation change merely by declaration.
That's courtesy of Obama. And recently the Supreme
Court said that it makes sense to them also in a split
decision. Truly propaganda at it's highest successful
saturation.

Joseph Goebbells of the Third Reich mesmerized
Germany with help from Adolph Hitler's charisma.

All they had were vacuum tube radios and out door stadiums. But they made the most of them and basically got the German people to commit mass suicide. Now with saturation bombardment with Hollywood films and twenty-four seven media pressure and the relentless guilt peddling many of the youth in this country don't feel confident about what sex they are and also feel they owe reparations to victims that they didn't enslave. Gay rights activists have hitched a ride on the African-American civil rights movement and conflated gays and black goals together. African-Americans do not think that's appropriate. I agree. Two different issues.

As it stands today because of the recent ruling by the Supreme Court, sexual orientation change can legally be created by a simple proclamation of the whim of the individual who feels and believes an inner voice. It's not an act of god or nature. It's an act of one person. Hollywood and god divorced after Cecil B. DeMille retired from Paramount.

And we all must give credence in a legal way, never mind if one doesn't believe the whimsy of another. Again, the heavy lifting has been done already. An important difference is the fact of physically mapping and editing genes is a process that can be patented when changing sexes or synthetically creating new sports on the human evolutionary tree. From that blueprint so to speak, money can be collected and the destiny of the human race can be altered in unknown ways.

Suffice to say the universal metaphysic of evolution is far different than the metaphysic of a business deal with monopoly money as the goal. What scientists edit out of the human genome and leave on the cutting room floor should be swept up and stored. Because we will find out what we cut will eventually have to be recreated—again.

That's a whole different set of boiler plate credibility that can bring law suits if not adhered to. It's similar to the draft sketch being built into a hard copy. Voila! It's a product. Then money can be charged. A great deal of money can be had by patenting gene editing configurations and putting a price for purchase along with it.

The promotion of gay subject matter and a new race is readily demonstrated by Facebook. Hollywood must have had a hand in pushing researchers and hall monitors at the company to proudly offer fifty-eight proper ID options or allowable salutations to the gay community for use on Facebook's platform. Those descriptions cover the letters in the LGBTQ+ acronym and fifty-two more which couldn't fit comfortably if one didn't want the readers mind to wander. Frankly any group that requires that much legalistic categorizing can't last or they will have to take themselves less seriously, simply because the defining of a person becomes so cumbersome that it will invite debate. Both gays and black civil rights activists do share one special trait that has helped them in their single purpose respective goals. That trait is—both lack a sense of humor. Maybe it's because money and power are more important to them than enjoying the facts of life.

Could all the courts in America go twenty-four seven because of acronym needs for litigation concerning possible trademark violation among members of acronym and their dealings with puzzled purveyors of goods and services? The Facebook employee who is in charge of ID'S on the FB platform has undergone Gender Reassignment Surgery. So he/she thinks he/she knows the subject. OK. Put it in writing. Not creative writing but legal writing so everyone knows what he/she is talking about. If that's possible.

How do courts and business parties interact with LGBers if the person in question sometimes is in doubt about their own sexual status at any given time?

There is one legal drawback if the human genome is edited or modified. The Civil Rights Act could lose the position of regulating the government entity. The Food And Drug Administration could legally be more appropriately the last word. The FDA regulates Genetically Modified Organisms (GMO). Maybe if the FDA takes over regulation, Hollywood could offer a cereal to get sex changed orally.

In addition to the considerable money that may flow, Hollywood gays could go beyond "tweaking" the genome. It's really only a matter of semantics for the slightly tweaked human to go to a full bodied new race. Hollywood ambition is Homeric. There is at least one recorded gene editing operation last year. The goal of the operation was to be immune to HIV/AIDS. That comes later in the book. I want to keep the plot in sequence and in context.

The recent Supreme Court ruling of protecting "sexual orientation "was an unexpected windfall. Protect "sexual orientation"? Interesting choice of words gambit. Protect from what? Some one else's preference or opinion? So "protect"necessarily takes protection of free speech and association from one so another can do what it wants to do in the areas of "sexual orientation". Can anyone define sexual orientation? When did the words sexual orientation enter the lexicon? What part of the thirteen billion and change age of the universe did "sexual orientation"- make its arrival known? Of course these questions are relatively naive. But "sexual orientation"is a rela- tively naive subject. Can't put ones finger on it if one can't find what part to finger. I think sexual orientation is a private issue and it doesn't deserve serious public consideration.

One potential problem for the gays rosey future could be when one gay individual tries to collect Social Security benefits payable to the same individ- ual but not the same "sexual orientation". So multiple checks would go out to the same address to differ- ently sexed individuals who are all actually still only one person. It takes ten years to fund social security benefits. Say the average age of a citizen tax payor is seventy. Allowing for some non working youth years, that allows maybe five checks for one person upon retirement using the LGBTQ+ menu of choices. Then and only then will congress will be moved to clarify the "sexual orientation"conundrum.

The conservatives didn't expect that ruling nor did the progressives. That reckless ruling will only embolden reckless Planet Hollywood gays. Planet comes from the Greek word meaning "wanderer". Wandering? Indeed. Like walking while wearing a blindfold?

Speaking of long term projects. Hollywood has increasingly seeped into mainstream politics. More oil spill than seep. Interestingly Dave Geffen raised eighteen million for the Clintons from the Hollywood crowd. Long before the Clintons, gays in Hollywood pushed for legislation like the Civil Rights Act Of 1964. They helped get it passed. Not satisfied with the initial described members of the protected groups in the Civil Rights Act, they are never satisfied, they lobbied for inclusion and specific protection for gays and the subsets succinctly represented by the acronym LGBTQ+. The + (plus)sign at the end of the acronym leaves the door purposely open depending on the results of aforementioned gene- editing experiments. It's like a legal term akin to reserving rights that are not listed but may become apparent later as new sprouts are identified and named.

Queer does as queer is, they are proud of the word queer. It's an in-your-face queer. It isn't a slur.

They earned and wanted the title. Exhibitionists both in film distribution and personality.

The Supreme Court recently gave the gays what they wanted. The Acronym was absorbed as a protected class. So now the protected classes add up to nine. They include race, color, religion, sex, national origin, physical disability, mental disability, reprisal and sexual orientation. Taken as a whole together with the preponderance of actual lawsuits brought in those areas of complaints as proof,the protected class of peoples under the umbrella of the Civil Rights Act now out number the unprotected. By definition the law that is supposed to protect minorities is now protecting a majority and discriminates against minorities. How's that for inappropriately named legislation? Looks like the straight white male is constructively the only class of people in the United States who are not protected from discrimination. The Civil Rights Act has already reached caricature. If freckled faced red heads are added as protected class I don't know what I will do.

How can there be a law that takes rights from one and gives those same rights to another? Sounds like a school yard game organized by nine or ten year old girls.

Our universe is made up of infinite entities. None are the same. None are equal. We and all those infinite entities are known by individual differences. The premise of the Civil Rights Act Of 1964 that all citizens should be treated as equal despite obvious differences cannot not be overlooked or made up by applying affirmative action. In the end, sooner or later, the law will have to be repealed to bring peace in the United States.

I think Hollywood moguls are behind the new race initiative. They also could have been behind persuading then mayor of San Francisco Gavin Newson to trash the custom of heterosexual marriage. The moguls could have also influenced President Obama in those "progressive values" executive orders.

One example of Obama's off-the-wall executive order was the order allowing choice or better put confusing youngsters about choosing what bathroom they should or could use. Obama also helped gays shore up their many medical bills from risky sex by getting the legislation passed known as the Affordable Care Act a.k.a. Obamacare. The act insures preexisting medical conditions like HIV/AIDS. Catch a disease in the morning. Sign up for insurance coverage before noon and have a better worry free afternoon. No insurance company can exist for long taking patients with preexisting medical conditions. And that includes our government assuming the losses. It will break the bank. Government enforced coverage of preexisting medical conditions skirts the issue of healthy living guide lines. It some what obviates a health code. Healthy living guide lines should not be a taboo topic. It's the gay way of putting legal boiler plate around their sexual personal antics. It's like getting the law to protect children from their scolding parents who warn of bad habits. Spoiled and bratty is a signature trait of the gays. Single payor insurance is the goal of gays and progressives. As of this moment they have got it.

And maybe now a new race is the next must have victory. Hollywood gays made contracting AIDS a kind of price to pay for love. Only Hollywood could try to turn a lethal pandemic into a love story. Although I don't think Bob Dylan would have written and sang a -rhyming- talking- sympathetic -lyric folk song about HIV/AIDS in one- long- breath- take. Come to think of it, Dylan was doing a form of rap. But to make a billion at rap like Jay-Z did, it must contain scatological references. Our culture has been trashed in the pursuit of equality. HIV/AIDS is the only disease in recorded history that has a special protected place in the greater family of non critical political progressives. What will they write about Geffen in one hundred plus years? Antichrist or freak of fiat money? Or an example of the beginning of the collapse of progressive politics. Or Dave Geffen, who?

Dave Gaffen's trivia includes as mentioned before his record company publishing a song written by cult leader and murderer Charles Manson. The song was performed by Axel Rose and Guns n' Roses. Rose thought Manson's infamous celebrity would be good for sales of his new album which had the Manson track. Geffen agreed. But Geffen Records had to return Manson's share of the profits, approximately sixty-two thousand dollars and change to the trust of a murdered victim. Can't make this stuff up.

How could Gaffen be so crude? Maybe because it was kind of deja vu when Geffen signed John Lennon in November nineteen eighty and then Lennon gets shot and killed in the next month. It made Geffen/ Lennon "Double Fantasy"album a huge hit. Maybe Geffen figures making money by some one getting killed or doing the killing can be good for business.

Thirteen and change billion years of evolution and the gays in Hollywood want a new race that can also make a huge income stream far into the future. What do they tell them at their bar mitzvah to get this kind of hubris?

Speaking of greedy humans and genome tinkering, it looks like one of us has come up with the first step in a three step process to create synthetic organisms. Dr. Craig Ventner and other Nobel Laureates have recently attempted this feat at the J. Craig Ventner Institute in Rockville, M.D. Dr. Ventner's goal is "to make artificial life forms with a minimum set of genes necessary for life. It is hoped that such organisms could one day be engineered to perform commercial tasks such as absorbing carbon dioxide from the air or churning out biofuels."

I suggest to the esteemed doctor that nature has already provided for accomplishing such a task. It's called a tree. And instead of replacing trees we should conserve them. Also the goal of reducing the genetic code to a "minimum"contradicts what nature says is best for species survival. Nature dictates that a plurality of genes is the reason species have evolved in an adaptive way. The species have all kinds of different genes to rely on. That's why our solar system is four and one half billion years old. It doesn't need to be perfected by a sixty thousand year old upstart—us. Here again nature provides multiple genes to do the chore naturally cleaning up the environment. And it will prevail. Gene editing will be constructively frowned on by nature. Eventually the gene editing jockeys will have to recreate through more gene editing the genes that they dismissed as not applicable or superfluous!

Of course if the doctor is only trying to raise money for his venture, the buzz words he uses alone could bring in twenty-five million in a heart beat.

By the way, instead of cleaning up pollution, a better choice would be not to create pollution. An example would be to walk more instead of driving.

Chapter II
Hollywood and San Francisco

The Hollywood Antitrust Case Of 1948 in fact changed the calculus for film making. For me I prefer pre-settlement movies to post- settlement movies. Pre-settlement produced more movies with more depth in the cast. More movies and income equals more additional movies. More of the chance of better movies and also bad movies but they kept coming. A windfall from the Settlement was individual stars became more valuable. Their name on the marquee could assure a measurable amount of income that was worth the risk of financing the film. Samuel Goldwyn regularly borrowed from A.P. Gianini's Bank Of America to finance a Goldwyn movie. Sam used his home as collateral. He took that risk because he had no theaters but the stars he hired and the story they told could be counted on to bring a certain amount of box office revenues.

Bernie Glows life's work became supercharged when a very lucrative expanded potential came into existence— —star power. The rest is history.

There are always newcomers for agents to look over. The newbies need the agent as much as the agent need talented people. Like a comet, Bernie glows with a tail of accrued wealth and celebrity. It's about maintaining and developing important connections. Make deals for those he represents and receive ten percent of what they get paid. For as long as the star gets paid. That's an annuity. That's nice. As the stars light brightens Bernie's percent share is reduced a little. But it stills flows. Name recognition is money in the bank. I have noticed that descendants of stars carry cachet with audiences. Agents are in a good position for success.

Only too many divorces could have set back or ruined Bernie. He had one divorce. He's now single. Bernie is a quick learner. He doesn't like to make the same mistake again. Hollywood agents are extremely important. A star can be spectacular but if no one knows or sees, it's a foggy night and it passes unnoticed. That's where Bernie comes in. He conjures a lens that he wants producers and directors to look through his lens and see his star sparkle. Bernie creates the lens with words and gestures. He knows when he is doing the lens correctly because he tracks the facial and body movements of the people he is trying to sell. He can sense if he's losing a chance of a contract but quickly uses a flying lead change and gallops ahead on a new track. He's a charmer of well cadenced always closing words.

I'm Mike Genoa. I was born and raised in San Francisco as were my parents. I was self employed and now retired from trading financial markets for over twenty years. I paint a little. I write a little. And mostly enjoy fencing competitively locally and nationally. I work out and open fence with club members two or three days a week in Oakland, California. I love fencing. Big sweat and it develops a calm approach to people and life. It delays getting old.

I think I fought in the Roman Colosseum in a previous life. It was in the early eighties with my wife I visited the Colosseum. We walked out on the higher level and looked down on the arena. I was overwhelmed with deja vu. Immediately it came to me. I was here once. I never lost with the sword. I retired early. And shortly after retirement, I died. For no apparent reason. But I felt there was nothing left to do that interested me so I left.

Back to the San Francisco story, the City is run by the virtual sons and daughters of Summer Of Love visitors who came and went but left their imprint behind—-for better or for worse. They are not the physical children of those long gone hippies many who died when they were young from self abuse. But they followed the hippies philosophy. What is the hippy philosophy? In a nutshell, if some one says "yes" the hippy answers "why"? Most of the hippies wouldn't say "no" with a follow-up explanation because most of the hippies didn't have an explanation. They just heard some other hippy use that "why" tactic maybe the night before and it worked. Or they thought it worked. Maybe the hippy that was overheard by the wannabe hippy was asking "why" he should try the mango espresso? So after sixty years the hippy philosophy in the city has become a caricature of it's former self. Imagine that if you can. I don't have to imagine. I live in San Francisco. Caricature comes with age but like age, caricature gets old.

San Francisco's enduring appeal and source of wealth comes from its limited geographical space, westerly winds from the nearby ocean and a moderate temperature. S.F.'s evolution is a metaphor for the unique experience of the Galapagos Islands. Both were removed from the norms of mainstream evolution and thus fostered a range of oddities. The Islands produced singular flora and fauna because of tectonic movements. San Francisco went curious because of talented entertainers cross breeding with bad tripping hippies who were protesting the Viet Nam War.

By the way war should only be declared by a national referendum vote in the positive. The Pentagon shape really to be more accurate should be changed to an inverted pentagram. They are evil. One example is their use of Agent Orange in the Viet Nam war and dropping napalm on humans and animals and the land and trees. One more example is all that atmospheric testing of nuclear bombs long after WWII was won.

Nobody could make this story up. It happened

a couple of years ago in the progressive enclave of Presidio Terrace in the city. The enclave is the most expensively valued in the city. It's about five blocks from where I live. I can see it from my roof where I could have an anchored tripod mounted for photos or any other chore that requires a steady support. It occurs to me that with all the facial recognition cameras at street level in the City the roofs maybe the one area of liberty. Times make the man and the plan. Under dire circumstances, I 'll bet I could escape from San Francisco by roof top easier than by driving my car—if it came to that. What would be the circumstances that would cause me to flee? I'll know it when I see it.

About two years ago an immigrant Chinese married couple were searching the web for real estate opportunities in San Francisco. Foreclosures can be once in a lifetime opportunities. But you have to put some tedious research time into it. And you have to know where to look. Tina Lam and Michael Cheng happened upon property for sale due to non payment of back taxes advertised by San Francisco City And County Tax Department. The bill was based on non payment of fourteen dollars ($14.00) a year. And what was the location, location, location of the delinquent property? It was Presidio Terrace. The Presidio Terrace Association failed to pay it's collective property tax on the common areas for thirty years. The couple paid ninety-thousand dollars ($90,000. 00) to clear arrears and penalties to secure title to the horseshoe shaped street and common areas including side walks in Presidio Terrace. That's it. Who knew? You find out by asking questions and searching.

Progressives dominate former and present occupants in the enclave. They include a home formerly owned by Senator Dianne Feinstein. Also Speaker Of The House Nancy Pelosi once resided there. Former Mayor Joseph Alioto once lived their also. During his tenure as mayor he had a difference of opinion with the Police Officers Association of the City. A bomb was planted and exploded at his front door of the mansion. The mayor settled with the union.

So with a list of wealthy former and present owners, no body thought anything bad could happen to them In the Presidio Terrace enclave. Many of the wealthy occupants of Presidio Terrace are attorneys or are in progressive politics. Consequently their greed consumes them to distraction. Maybe the progressives residents were distracted with reaching out to illegals. Or maybe visiting members of the LGBTQ+ community, who might have an itch that they wanted the progressives to scratch for them. Or maybe taking a shopping list or nursing all the rest of those cause celebre people who were either in costume or just being their odd natural self with all those expensive special needs.

But something indeed happened overnight. The home owners found out through the mail that barbarians had seized the only street in Presidio Terrace. Not through soldiers and tanks. But off-the-shelf attorneys did the chore quietly like a boa constrictor snake. Lawyers are kind of like snakes and that's giving the worst of the comparison to the reptile. At least the snake has skin in the game. Lawyers don't pay if they lose. We need a "loser pays" mechanism in our tort proceedings. The United States is the only country on the planet that doesn't have one. Now back to the story. How did this seizure happen? How will they get their property back? Maybe the Chinese couple could slipped in with the notification of property transfer a survey that was to be filled out by the enclave residents about the desirability of having a once a week live /wet market street sale in Presidio Terrace ? Eels in tanks, chickens in cages, bats in boxes, reptiles and insects doubled up in animal carrying cases—ugh.

First rule of governing: Control and keep safe for all the people the common areas. The Chinese couple dreams were dashed. The Board Of Supervisors interceded and disallowed the sale. There was no legal reason for the Boards decision. It was just a-in-the-daylight-high-handed-illegal judgment.

Part of San Francisco's history is it's anti-war stance during the nineteen sixties. While we all are waiting for a National Referendum whether to go to war or not go to war or, here's a gambit to slow the rush to war. Conscientious objector is a legitimate excuse as per military regulations to refuse deployment to a war zone as a combatant. Armed service members are citizens also. They have a right to say how their life is to be lived and what it could be sacrificed for what objective. War for its own sake is a criminal act. Frivolous commanders and politicians starting wars or getting involved in wars that are not a threat to our national security are constructively grounds for manslaughter and murder. Murder not only to opposing armies but also to our own troops. Hey troops. Just tell your commanders and reps in congress that you don't want to be a part of forever wars. A recent example is our quasi declaration of war on Iran. Sanctioning a country so it can't carry on normal commerce is an act of war. We embargoed Japan and got ourselves in the second world war and went on to bomb Nagasaki and Hiroshima with two nuclear bombs. Pentagon could be proud of their mission accomplished in that crime. But most of America has grown up and matured while the Pentagon generals are still stuck in a primitive mind and in the mud. As they said in the sixties, "Suppose they gave a war and nobody showed up?"

The Pentagon always want another war in Mideast. About a year ago a Japanese oil tanker was suspiciously attacked by unknown actors in the Straits Of Hormuz. It was timed for the arrival of Japanese Prime Minister Shinzo Abe who was in Tehran seeking to diffuse the dangerous situation between the U.S. and Iran that was started by our unilateral withdrawal from the international nuclear agreement with Iran. Within minutes Secretary Of State Pompeo blamed Iran. That's a stretch given the circumstances of a diplomatic peace meeting between Iran and Japan who both were signatories to the international nuclear treaty.

Why rush to war? What about our troops? Our troops are also citizens. No commander has the authority to be reckless with their well being. If a commander is reckless then the troops have a justifiable recourse to protect themselves. In this situation we would yet again dive into another deadly and costly war against an historically traceable Iran —- Persia. It's a real country with a rich culture. It shouldn't be the object of a reckless Neocon foreign policy. Or a money-making business for the military-industrial complex. Or for the protection of Saudi Arabia which was kind of created/recreated by The Standard Oil Of California when it discovered oil there in nineteen thirty-three.

Or to protect Israel which was a United Nations 1947 creation. Israel is not worth it. Besides it has 200 nukes. If we are worried about nukes in the Mideast. Start with that rogue state.

Israel receives yearly over two and one half billion in cash from the United States. It is alleged by the Council For The National Interest that ten percent ($250,000,000) of that sum finds it way back into Israels U.S. lobbying efforts. The scheme according to the CNI has Israel directing the funds through one hundred and twenty-six PACs with unrelated names to Israel. That staggering sum is over 11% of yearly lobbying funds spent by all the other lobbyists combined!

AIPAC and other pro-Israel lobbies should not enjoy access to our Congress as if they are a 51st state. With less money and influence in America, Israel would be forced to make peace and stop murdering Palestinians.

The Foreign Lobby Registration Act would expose and end the spider-web of Israeli influence. The Council for the National Interest is pushing to have Israel open its books as required by The Foreign Lobby Registration Act. So far it's still in the inbox gathering dust.

I have personally witnessed one of the Israel controlled PAC'S in action. While sharing office space and fax machines with a hedge fund almost twenty-five years ago, a fax communique was mis-delivered to me instead of the fund next door. It was addressed to a northern California improvement club. The sender was a person or entity in Israel.

Chapter III
Man And Superman

Man is the eager tool maker, it includes language and money as tools. He makes or changes laws as fast as objects can come off a conveyor built. He can't wait for evolution. He wants leveraged buy outs now, pronto, on the hop as soon as possible.

Many of mans new laws or cultural habits are in direct conflict with our four and one half billion year solar system laws. One example would be pollution. A fall out from the manufacturing process is pollution. It kills other organisms so that man might make money. Our impact on earth is akin to the impact of diabetes on a body.

All the laws we have on the books now have an implied expiration date because of the implied demands our presumptuous laws and mans greed require. A kind of shelf life. Our laws are net takers of natural resources. We can't afford presumptuous laws or products that go against the ability of the planet to fulfill the demand. Natural laws have successfully worked for four and a half billion years. Ignore those unwritten laws at risk of peril.

Wall Street for example creates wealth via stock initial public offerings (IPO). Overnight the IPO is valued in the billions. Those billions only have value if they can buy something. A mansion? A exotic car? Rare wooded furniture for a large living room? A private plane? A private yacht? All those expensive things come from scarce and dwindling natural resources. They cannot be replaced. Of all the dwindling resources, water and fresh air and wild lands are the most valuable. They support our species and a riot of other living things. We shouldn't plunder the common heritage of the planet for vanity and trinkets. Do we deserve the light bulb? Prometheus thought so. But man created Prometheus. So Prometheus is not a reliable reference. Wall Street inhabitants need a kind of humane rodenticide to check their ambitions.

New born babies cry. Hint of things to come? People who were born yesterday, speaking of their mental abilities, usually become misanthropes before noon of the next day. I believe it's about population. There is an inverse relationship between the number of too many people crowded into areas and the pleasure of their company.

How many humans should be optimum to mitigate that inverse relationship? The classic ages of humans was roughly a time line starting with the Egyptians in 3000 B.C. through the Babylonians and Chinese and on to the Assyrians and Persians and then the Greeks and then the Romans. I'm sure there are others who are noteworthy but I'm more interested in what the approximate collective population of those societies were and their impact on the natural world. Everything leaves a foot print. What are we getting that's worthwhile for our footprints?

According to Wikipedia the worlds inhabitants totaled about 250 -500 million in those classic eras. That population number should be our goal. I think the world would become wonderful at that level of human occupation.

Fast forward to the early 1970's when our numbers were approximately 3.7 billion. At that level of occupancy we noticed a collapse in fish stocks in the wild and the extinctions of flora and fauna in inhabited areas. Safely said that the animals that we kill and eat and the resources that we humans now despoil for our frivolous utility have better pedigrees and are more rare than the humans that consume them.

Now we are looking at 8 billion fun-seeking and hungry humans who all want. That want can't be satiated without rendering what we see everyday becoming unrecognizable soon. Forget the prophets and the good books ? No. They still have wisdom which could be a guide book for the health and sustainability of the environmental. But on a day to day basis, a kind and gentle misanthropy will be more helpful in designing a future. Not suggesting harming anyone. But more along the lines of incentives via the tax code to limit births. Also transfer of great wealth from those that have to those that don't have via purchasing procreation ability from agreeing people.

What part will gadgets play? I think less gadgets and more personal value added will make some people indispensable and large swaths of others redundant. Gadgets have degraded natural selection and prolonged stagnation in individual thinking. Man with his clever inventive brain has put himself out of work. Machines have replaced the inventors relentlessly and silently. Homo sapiens?

Glance at a world map. There is approximately one hundred and eighty-nine countries. Natural evolution came up with that disposition of countries and tribes all by itself. The Civil Rights Act Of 1964 constructively disallows the quasi segregation of the one hundred and eighty-nine countries. The Act is the most presumptuous law in thirteen billion and eight hundred million years.

And man made the law up fifty-six years ago. Repeal the law. Simply civil rights cannot be had if it takes the civil rights away from some one and gives the same civil rights to some one else. And in todays application of the law there are more protected classes than unprotected classes. Which fact by itself is the definition of discrimination and unequal status before the law. Obviously a badly written law that gunsling attorneys have used to their advantage and in fact exacerbated racial friction.

America's grand experiment of equality for all,and never mind the contribution of each, ignores and mocks the metaphysics of a sustainable social paradigm. Also the euphemism of "multiculturalism" clashes with a quick glance of any globe or world map. All those countries that make up the quilt of the planet are positive proof that people and countries are different. Which fact by extension argues more for a segregated society rather than a integrated one. That is in general and there are exceptions in symbiotic societies.

It follows that our United States will eventually split up and fracture along racial and philosophical contours. One size fits all never worked.The European Union is another example of an abomination that will lose it's shape and purpose. The individual parts like France, Greece, Italy, Germany etc will once again makes themselves unique. The filthy glue of the Euro will vanish along with the dollar. Individual countries will rely on integrity and fair commerce to exist. In a word barter will be the ultimate exchange medium. The ancient countries in Europe will come through the mist and gloom of one government for diverse races to a place where diverse races have their own government based on personal choice and their own segregated land. Not on some thieving politician and the roving attorneys who work on commission to keep the citizens in line.

The headquarters for the European Union is in Brussels, Belgium. How about members of the Union each send a raiding party to Brussels a la King Alaric and his Visigoths sack of Rome in 410 C.E. and sack the EU buildings?

Simply, governments worldwide and in particular our own United States who enforce social engineering laws that are financed by fiat money will in the end repeal civil rights laws and stop printing monopoly money and resort to one large loud speaker. That's if they want to remain in power. Count on it.

Speaking of differences, some years ago, I competed in a fencing tournament in Miami, Florida. I shared a lunch counter with a Jewish, Russian-born, divorce-attorney female. We talked a bit. Our waiter was a recent, Cuban-born immigrant male.

After that brief encounter, I am convinced that if that woman and that man were to marry, the possible proportional distribution of their collective genes could produce the Antichrist.

Former President Barack Obama is/was the literal incarnation of President Lyndon Johnson's Great Society social engineering laws that influenced our culture to this day. President Obama was born in 1961. That was roughly the start of the Civil Rights movement. But it was sometime after the start of loose living, drugs and racial and gender sexual experimentation.

Obama's hereditary daddy was some black dude from Kenya. Obama's mommy was some eager white gal from Kansas. Daddy went on to other eager gals and mommy just went on. So who raised Obama? Well if he's like most other people or organisms he would be influenced and somewhat raised by his surroundings. These influences include his state, his schools and the morals, customs and politics of the times.

President Lyndon Johnson was in office between 1963 to 1969. Johnson fathered the Great Society which include massive expansions of the federal influence in private lives. These oversized and expensive expansive influences took the form of Medicare, Civil Rights legislation, voting laws, immigration laws and an expansion of the Viet Nam War. Were the policies and legacies of Lyndon Johnson a quasi artificial insemination of all the Obama type children that followed? Is Barack Obama part natural and part government fathered? Is Barack Obama a legal/cultural product of daddy # 2 Lyndon Johnson?

So what's the future? If Barack is an example, then this new race of the Great Society- effected children will be a spoiled group who will be very expensive to maintain.

Barack Obama is plural man.

America is nothing if not diverse. Barack Obama is the perfect template for progressive diverse identity politics. He's a throwback to central casting in the studio system. I swear there must have been others who were quietly being compared to Obama by the back room boys and girls who run the Democratic Party. But Obama was chosen and groomed. He checked all the boxes. The perfect candidate for selling the product of diversity. In a word"synthetic" comes to mind as a description of Obama.

When in office the media would edit out his mistakes and spin it so the republicans looked like the ones who screwed up. Main stream media and the edit scissors is better than lying in an article. Because the editor uses actual targeted people but misrepresents and clips their message and words. All quotes are necessarily out of context. And the media quotes part of the quote which is a lie.

Obama is one half black and one half white which reflects the increasing interracial relationships in the U.S.. He was born and raised in Honolulu, Hawaii which gives him Pacific Islanders credentials. He spent part of his youth living in Indonesia which gives him Asian bona fides. His religious background includes an estranged Muslim father who turned atheist and a Christian mother. That pretty much covers most religious persuasions. His father left Barack and his mother so Barack was raised in a single parent household niche. That works in America. Our own welfare system selects for single parent. Obama studied law at Ivy League Harvard. So he can brag of a sliver of elitism. He was a teacher. The teachers union is the largest contributor to the democratic party. He served as an Illinois State Senator and was a U.S. Senator representing Illinois. Experienced politician also. He's married and a father of two and wrote two books and "inhaled".

Fiscal irresponsibility picked up speed with George W. Bush and continued through Barack Obama's second term. We got Obama because we had George W Bush. In a word Bush was and is a "moron".

The U.S. had approximately sixteen years of federal deficits and Federal Reserve Quantitative Easing adding up to one trillion per year. Then came Donald Trump and the Federal Reserve Quantitative Easing squared. The zeros are more like open mouth gasping surprises—-more like a chorus of emoji. Or the zeros could be like the bubbles in our stock market and bond market and in the number of the population.

Now we are well into a full two generations of an unreal economic expectation and experience. This trip has never been experienced by any generation of peoples in recorded history. I dare say that our four and one half year old solar system hasn't a similar example of individual organisms trying to change the metaphysics of how life works. Or in a thirteen and one half billion year old universe which includes the Big Bang. Infinite metaphysics had logic and regularity of change. Homo sapiens decided it was in its power to fix outcomes so human laws worked. Preposterous. In our own infancy sixty thousand years ago, people created value and wealth the old fashioned way. They worked and saved. Now congress and the executive along with judicial activism and the federal reserve mandate fiat money be created to support the brave new world of equality. Equality before the law and increasingly equality in results. We had deficits before. But on a much smaller scale. Notably the Lyndon Johnson presidency. At that time Johnson and Congress funded the Viet Nam War and an expansion of entitlements without regard to how they were to be paid. Three people raised in that poorly thought out period were the same George W. Bush and the same Barack Obama and now Donald Trump. They saw. They experienced. They copied exponentially.

What will the eighteen years and counting experience of trillion dollar plus deficits coupled with trillion dollar plus Federal Reserve purchases of government securities do to young and immature minds? Will the young minds vote for additional zeros added on to the already numerous zeros? Will Bush and Obama and Trump look frugal in comparison going forward?

Money was our tool. But our tool has become us. Use a tool lose your place?

One thing for sure. Afghanistan will not change as much compared to what the U.S. will experience in change in the coming years.

In 193 A.D. Didius Julianus out bid the former emperors family and bought the position of Caesar from the Praetorian Guard. Pertanix was the former Emperor who wanted a strong fiscal policy and hard currency. The Praetorian Guard killed Pertanix because citizens didn't want belt tightening. Didius Julianus offered more money to every member of the Praetorian guard and so he was proclaimed Emperor by the Praetorian Guard. He promptly devalued the Roman currency to pre Pertanix values. Fiat currency versus hard currency was the issue. But the Praetorian Guard who were paid in hard currency were insulted by the immediate devaluation by Didius Julianus. So the Praetorian Guard immediately killed Didius Julianus in spite. D.J. ruled for only three months. The Praetorian Guard was as fickle a ten year old girl.

Relying on fiat money as a way of life for individuals or empires is a failed policy. Like the word policy almost spells police but it doesn't, the discipline of law enforcement eventually goes away when the currency becomes phony.

So here we all our some two thousand years later still dealing with the fall out of fiat money and debt and the impact on citizens of Rome and for that matter the greater empire. It's always about money. No matter what any one says. Also the military runs the political show. One thing to look forward to is the greed and arrogance eventually consumes the politicians and the military to the point they start killing each other. I like it. There is an upbeat song appropriate for this eventuality it is titled "Look For The Silver Lining". Jerome Kern did the music and Buddy DeSylva did the lyrics.

P.S. The military will win over the politicians in

the end. As recounted above the armed forces allow the politicians to make policy but the real policy is to pay the armed forces and they will let the politicians go through the motions of having power ... until the money runs out.

P.P.S. The final battle will be when the militias around the country take on the military for the ultimate determination of with whom power resides in the United States

P.P.P.S. After the power struggle is resolved there will be necessarily another rearranging of the map of the United States. There could be two outcomes. If the military wins there will not be individual states, The U.S. will become "The State". United will be dropped. If the militia wins then the fifty states will slowly become closer to the one hundred and eighty-nine countries map on the world globe. I favor the latter considering how different we all are.

Chapter IV
Mike's Background & Speculations

I was taught by the Jesuits at Saint Ignatius College Preparatory High School. While there I was never approached by a predator clergy . I'm aggressive by nature so if there were any predators in the clergy they stayed hidden in their dark speculative thoughts waiting for an unambiguous prey.

I went on to the University Of San Francisco to study philosophy. Left after two years to work at the Pacific Coast Stock Exchange as a self employed trader on the floor. It was a ball. But after a while it gets old like I got older. Much physical energy was used along with the stress of competition. Between Saint Ignatius and University Of San Francisco I was exposed to classical subjects that I revisited later in life. It was a very rewarding and comforting education. Aristotle said, "Philosophy in good times serves as an ornament. In bad times philosophy is a refuge". I personally have been increasingly moved to put my life experiences in the context of evolution or change. Not in the context of time. Because time is a construct of man. Change or evolution is more accurate than time.

The Jesuits at Saint Ignatius and University Of San Francisco also offered theology as a course. It was more than offered it was a requirement. On the subject of God and Jesus being the Son Of God, I here speculatively compare the formation of the Catholic religion to the riots in Chicago in nineteen sixty-eight at the Democratic National Convention and the spectacle of the Chicago Seven at that convention. That event largely represented the birth and strength of the anti-war movement in America. Notably we are in more wars now since then and we don't have the draft. The difference is the enormous effects of mountains of fiat money and debt that fuels forever wars. In war we trust. With or without the citizens approval. We need a National Referendum On War. Thumbs up or thumbs down. No group in power should have the power to declare war by themselves. We can't trust any one with that enormous power. Troops should withhold their service unless the reasons are justified.

In the wake of the riots came other cultural changes and movements that would change the United States forever. These included the environmental movement and American-style socialism with expected and unexpected applications of the newly passed Civil Rights Act Of 1964 legislation.

The poster group for the counter-culture rioters in Chicago were the Chicago Eight later to become the Chicago Seven when Black Panther Bobby Seale had a separate trial. The Group was made up of activist, socialist/communist Jews, black, Irishmen, and Wasps. It had broad appeal. The leader was Jerry Rubin. The message was anti-government,anti-war, anti-establishment, anti-business, anti-critical thinking and some would add anti-personal hygiene. Despite the mostly unsustainable agenda, the group and others did change the course and culture of America. Subsequently President Nixon did stop the Draft and other politicians were elected to office as anti-war representatives.

So with some clever editors who wanted to create a religion which also could double as a hidden political movement trying to control behavior of people now and in the hereafter — —in about four hundred years from now—the same elapsed time between a living Christ and the story of his life as per the Bible written by then techno-clerics who also held positions of power in what was left of the Roman Empire—- could Mayor Daly become a kind of Roman governor like Pontus Pilate and the scene of the riot at Lincoln Park become the spot where Judas betrayed Jesus and was subsequently crucified? Could the Chicago seven be like the twelve Apostles? Could Jerry Rubin be a more modern day clear -the-temple- anti-establishment Jesus? Is this the way the Catholic Church stumbled into existence? How ever it came about, it spread compliments of Rome's ubiquitous system of roads. All roads led to Rome. It was by necessity a two-way street that Rome found out the hard way and the down side of Christ's socialism.

It has been said that people of the Book (ancient scriptures with a common root source) are to be respected and honored in their beliefs. The Book(s) that are referenced include the Bible, Koran and Torah. These books represent the foundations for three religions-Christian, Islamic and Jewish respectively.

It has also has been noticed by many that people of the Book are the ones mainly involved in regional and world wars throughout history. Is there a connection? Maybe if people of the Book were to read and believe to some degree other books to offset their preoccupation with the one Book of their respective religions then there would be some mitigation of the Book-sourced wars that keep happening over and over and over and over and over and over.

While we are here. The Bibles Book of Genesis, Chapter I, Verse 27-28 says "And God created man to his own image, to the image of God he created him. Male and female he created them. And God blessed them saying increase and multiply and fill the earth and subdue it and rule over the fishes of the sea and the fowls of the air and all creatures that move upon the earth".

Indeed. And man did do these things. But so effectively was mans zeal that eighty percent of ocean fish stocks have disappeared. Certain U.S. domestic bird populations have plummeted a similar eighty percent. And creatures that move upon the earth have lost their habitat, have been killed off for fun, have been run over in haste, have been poisoned by mercury from mans fossil fuel addiction.

Genesis, Chapter I, verse 31, further states, "And God saw all the things that he had made and they were very good".

How about Three Gorges Dam becoming the worlds largest cesspool? How about the slaughter of dolphins and whales in Japan? How about pollution being created by the hand of God? Those example are not good god work according to plan in my view.

Personally I want peace with nature and I want the other creatures to have peace also. It wasn't only people of the Book that followed Gods counseling and polluted the earth but other people not of the Book also created pollution. How about everyone putting down books of instructions and learn to look and judge personally what a better place could be created if balance was the goal instead of some religious fairy tale for people who are afraid of the dark.

How about this comment on religion? Jerusalem is the semitic city of three religions. Judaism, Islam and Christianity have important historical sites in Jerusalem. Jews have the remains of their temples. Islam has the Dome of The Rock where Mohammed supposedly ascended into heaven. The Christians revere Jerusalem as a place where Jesus taught. They were all Semitic. The eighteen century German philosopher Arthur Schopenhauer said, "A Semite is the master of the lie." But Schopenhauer never met twenty-first century politicians or The Clintons.

Many Semites ended up in Hollywood. I think there is a connection between selling tickets to fantasy movies and cartoons in between and selling religious indulgences. All are thin on credibility.

The fact remains concerning Schopenhauer's remark about Semites and his opinion of their veracity. There are three religions from one semitic area? What odds on that fact? Three creators of the universe all from a little dusty town that their followers may periodically suffer from the heat?

Interestingly the first pope of the Catholic Church was a Jew named Peter. And that's also the last Jew to be called a pope.. All the popes that followed were approved by the Emperors of Rome. Nero, the first emperor to constructively control the Catholic Church wanted to be emperor in the secular and the religious worlds.

The story is covered in a entertaining fashion by Barry Leonardini in his book titled, Jesus Was Tall And Well Spoken: A Different Account Of Christ And His Catholic Church.

I don't believe in god. My creed is the golden rule. If I had a religion it would be based on good stewardship of the environment.

In other words, we all have an innate knowledge of what's right and what's wrong.

It would seem that in man's evolution and with his addiction to tools which include language and money, man has stopped listening to the inner voice and overruled fairness with arrogance and greed. Use a tool lose your place. Stay close to the ways of nature. It doesn't mean living on dirt floors. Also it doesn't mean living in twenty thousand square feet homes.

The Big Bang was approximately thirteen and one half billion years ago. Our solar system and our earth are approximately four and one half billion years old. So how did we get by when we only found out about our gods two thousand years ago? And then when we named and worshiped our particular gods we started killing each other. Forget gods. Enjoy the day.

San Francisco politics is solidly sixties heritage. Board Of Supervisors have laid down some laws that confuse people who are looking for threads of logic as to an underlying theme. Some examples : No smoking in public but if one needs a needle for heroin injections they are available at no cost compliments of the city. What happens to the needles? They are discarded. There are bags for the used needles that the city makes available. S.F. logic! Expect drug addicts to be responsible with discarded hypodermic needles. San Francisco has a Board Of Health for restaurants.

Yet lets people sleep on the sidewalks and permits biological necessities by those same people in the open.

Some years ago when now Governor Gavin Newson was Mayor of San Francisco a tragic event occurred. San Francisco's Sanctuary City policy is at best bratty and ill-mannered. At worst it's a government sponsored criminal- enterprise that aids law breakers to avoid justice. The ultra-liberal city policy flows from the cities wealth. Mayor Newson didn't formulate the policy. But he's certainly the incarnation of an overindulgent brat. He's the product of a no-talent family who's only achievement was to have parlayed Gordon Getty's windfall inheritance money into a political family business. Gav's the poster boy of a progressive political philosophy that is created by the power of money and connections looking for more money and more power.

The downside of a bratty and ill-mannered sanctuary city philosophy was recently recorded. Suspected murderer Edwin Ramos is thought to have senselessly killed Tony Bologna and his two sons over a right of way traffic problem. It turns out that bratty Ramos had a long criminal record and could have been deported long ago if the cities policies were not skewed to helping the undeserving.

Newsom is a brat for ignoring the law. Ramos is a brat for ignoring the law.

It was said that 19th century Irish immigrants

when entering a new country asked one question first, "What kind of government you got here ? Because I'm against it." Mayor Newsom is a descendant of that kind of political Irish stock. He's the mayor that launched homosexual marriage in San Francisco. His criminal behavior redefined the cultural custom of marriage. He probably handed George Bush the margin of votes to win. Newsom should have been impeached. But he is the Platonic sodomite of the homosexual community in S.F.

Well he doubled-down with his Irish anarchy. He and S.F.'s Board of Supervisors urged San Francisco's law enforcement agencies not to comply with criminal provisions of any new federal immigration bill. Newsom said, "If people think we were defiant in the gay marriage issue, they haven't seen defiance." Wow. Why all the venom? What's his problem? Why would he want to protect criminals? Because he has a way that the illegals can one day vote?The main reason why he became mayor was together with his father Judge William Newsom Jr. they do a courtier-like performance for billionaire Gordon Getty. Getty's money and the judges contacts got former Mayor Willie Brown to appoint Gavin to the Board of Supervisors. From there Gavin and groupies developed a cheap version of J.F.K. including a striking rent-a-wife and an unfurnished home in the required political district.

Since Gavin is such an Irish caricature of rebellion he should resort to drinking to temper his raging spirit. Seriously, other Irish playwrights, poets, actors and characters have somewhat civilized themselves under the influence of alcohol. If one can't stand being normal or one really doesn't get it then one should fake it.

Chapter V
San Francisco Trivia

Here's a San Francisco example of aging into a caricature. San Francisco is the place where only two people are required to establish a political party or unique culture. If one wanted to compare San Francisco to a restaurant it would be similar to a Drive-through McDonalds. Order from an extensive menu of what is possible in the City By The Bay and they will bag it and you wont have to pay. See you next time and drive away. Want more. Just vote progressive. That's the only cost and what's hidden in that bargain. Whether one wants to sleep on the sidewalks or shoot up in the park or change genders, just get a friend legal or not and you are a political force. You will be shoe-horned into S.F. culture between illegals who came last night and car jackers who are released this morning because what they stole from the car was less than a thousand dollar threshold of a felony. Of course if you can get a pro bono attorney then the TWO requirement is waived.

The San Francisco yellow pages are largely filled with lawyer address' and phone numbers. Lawyers are akin to gun-for-hire trouble shooters. They can be had with no money down. Only agree to a contingency law suit. Those kind of law suits include as much as forty percent pay out to the attorney as his fee. It's a license to steal. It's "legal" extortion. The antidote to this thievery is "loser pays"in law suits. The United States is the only country that does not have a loser pays procedure. The reason why dates back to pre-American Revolution. It's related to suing Britain and King George when we were a colony. King George is gone. But greedy attorneys are still thriving with their gun slinging.

The attorney section in the San Francisco Yellow Pages is larger than any other category or in some cases combinations of many different categories. One could have plumbers and electricians and hospitals and auto repairs and accountants bundled and still have a plurality of lawyers left over. According to the latest edition of the San Francisco Yellow Pages, there are forty pages listing attorneys. Notably in those same Yellow Pages, a cumulative thirty-six pages of life's necessities are listed in smaller increments: Appliances: three pages ; Clothes: five pages ; Electricians: five pages ; Engineers: four pages ; Grocers: four pages ; Plumbing: thirteen pages and Hospitals: two pages. They all add up to thirty-six pages. So you have some change left over. Maybe you want an accountant which are listed on four pages

Why do we have all these lawyers compared to the meager percentages of necessary professions and vendors? I think there are two main reasons. The first is the lure of money, lots of money whether the attorney wins the case or loses the case or settles the case. Government pays "pro bono" lawyers. Consequently there is a powerful incentive to sue. The United States is the only country that doe not have "loser pays" in litigation. Tort reform is long over due to address this license to steal. The legal system is so costly because of its built-in systems of legal complicating procedures that continually puts arriving at a resolution into another month or year. "Oh Good'ee choir the attorneys ". The second reason follows from the first. Since "according to the law" requires attorneys to track the maze of instructions codified in juris prudence, one need only be a good map reader, greedy and not much value-added in planning. The only creative skill required is writing the brief of grievances. Brief writing in legal cases usually fall into the fiction category.

Follow these instructions and many expensive billable hours will follow. The result is off-the -shelf newly graduated JD's (Juris Doctors) thrive at every one else's expense.

Twenty-five percent of my 1961 high school graduating class went on to become lawyers. One half of those attorneys would steal a hot stove. The other half would watch and learn.

Attorney hourly rates are reaching fifteen hundred dollars per hour. Attorney fees have been climbing six to seven percent per year for the past five years. Meanwhile the average American workers salary has been stuck at around eighteen dollars per hour for those past five years losing out to inflation. Also during this past five years, the price of one nine millimeter shell has hovered around ten cents each.

When access to justice is only available to the wealthy through the wealthy, evolutionary experience predicts a low-cost alternative will evolve.

Last year Purdue Pharma declared bankruptcy. Thousands of law suits forced a legal cease fire to count assets and the liabilities.

Purdue Pharma's OxyContin is the drug that has been abused by thousands of addicted people. Those people "caused" the opioid crisis not the Federal Drug Administration which approved the drug OxyContin. Any law suit should have been directed at the drug addicts since they are the criminals. Of course that won't happen. Because in this era of progressive law suits attorneys need a victim. Never mind that the victim is actually the criminal. Fact is there were no laws broken except by the doctors who wrote prescriptions for OxyContin irresponsibly without regard to the drugs danger for addiction. That's how legal reasoning should have gone. But this is not about legality. This is about making money for immoral and greedy legal workers.

OxyContin requires a prescription written by a doctor. Once that legal requirement is fulfilled, Purdue Pharma legally is out of the line of fire. The docs are next in line legally. If so, why weren't doctors sued for irresponsible prescription writing? Because thousands of law suits against thousands of doctors would take time. There's less money in suing individual doctors. For the thousands of attorneys in the class action against Purdue Pharma, Purdue is a convenient one stop drive buy shake down and settlement.

How would Purdue be viewed by that roving pack of legal dogs if it denied OxyContin to certain victims and they in turn contacted an attorney for help in securing pain relief? How would an attorney respond to a plea for help in dealing with pain.

Another drug related crime at the national level shows just how Big Pharma and our legal system are a big part of our lives. From the local doctor to the federal government including possibly influencing our foreign policy in far away Afghanistan.

In 2018 Martin Shkreli was sentenced to eight years in prison. Leading up that closure is an interesting sequence of events. The F.B.I. says he was running a Ponzi scheme. The vehicle was MSMB Capital Management. It is a hedge fund run by Shkreli. He says that's a red herring charge. He maintains that his raising the price of sixty year old drug Daraprim from $13.50 per tablet to $750.00 per tablet is the real reason for his arrest. Shkreli through his hedge fund took over Turing Pharmaceuticals which had the Daraprim patent and jammed the price hike. Who feels sorry for Shkreli? I don't. But the anatomy of this sequence of events is enlightening. Who created and empowered Shkreli? The Federal Reserve created Shkreli. Because of quantitative easing and zero interest rates over the prior ten years, he and others have had full use of cheap money to fulfill a greedy persons fantasy. But all dreamers are awakened at some point to reality.

Pfeizer, Glaxo, Merck etc are our drug lords. They pay billions over the years to our congress so they can deal drugs in America. They have hooked so many naive people on drugs that they have spawned the Mexican Drug cartels to fill the demand. So there's the government again. Federal Reserve then power of big Pharma through big government.

This brings to mind the eighteen year old war the United States has been involved in Afghanistan. Bin Laden was killed in 2011. This was because of his master minding 9/11. Our government took ten years to dispatch Osama. But Shkreli wanders into Big Pharmas space and the roof caves in within weeks, within weeks! Afghanistan is the nexus of Big Government, the military-industrial-complex and I think I can include Big Pharma. Afghanistan produces ninety percent of heroin in the world. Heroin is de facto a cheap knock off of OxyContin and other pain-killers that Big Pharma peddles on TV and all media in 185 languages. Do you think that opium eradication is a American values goal or more specifically a Big Pharma's goal?

Before there was Big Government and Big Pharma it was less complicated. Let's use aspirin as an example of how some drugs began. Edward Stone of Oxford University in 1763 analyzed willow bark. Willow bark was used for thousands of years for human ailments by indigenous peoples. Stone found Acetylsalicylic Acid to be the active ingredient in the bark. Years later Bayer of Germany synthesized the acid and put it into a bottle and the rest is history. Maybe the whole endeavor cost a couple hundred thousand? That includes manufacturing capability which includes packaging.

Some years ago Tufts Center For The Study of Drug Development issued the results of its study of modern day drug introduction costs. It said it costs about $2.5 billion to bring a new drug to market. Well if the history of the aspirin is any guide and taking into account inflation since 1763, I reckon that $2.4 billion is spent for unreadable lab tests and packaging design and legal costs associated with disclaimers and $100 million in copying what nature provides for free in jungles and everyones backyards. Everyone has a well paid job to cure a headache and create another headache.

The headache isn't unique to America. Japan has a coming headache also. It's Big Pharma space is offering a new cancer fighting drugs for one hundred and forty-three thousand dollars for a yearly treatment. Per capita income in Japan is approximately thirty-seven thousand dollars. Looks like many will be disappointed. Our own U.S. recently approved Sovaldi for eighty-four thousand dollars per treatment. It's for Hepatitus C. Our own per capita income is fifty-three thousand dollars. Math doesn't work out for average people. Of course Big Pharma is counting on the government to come up with the difference. So it's not so much the cost of ingredients or advertising that drive up the price as much as how much can Pharma charge and get away with. With the help of our government.

San Francisco claims to be progressive and caring. Abuse of power and self dealing are not the advertised goals of progressive politics. But using the false flag of caring is an easy way to get into boarding and raiding range of the U.S ship of state. Speaker of The House Nancy Pelosi and husband Paul together with Senator Dianne Feinstein and husband Dick Blum are a progressive juggernaut. They use a Red Cross flag of a hospital ship instead of the more truthful Jolly Roger on a legally outfitted ship-of-the line government property raider. They spend roughly half the day working for the government duties that are legit and the other part of the day boarding and raiding . They have made hundreds of millions for their own families and other investors in their family's business of private equity investments by self dealing and abuse of power in selling off U.S. government property.

Ever deal with the federal government? Most of the time you are either on perma-hold or the governments website is down. No problem for Feinstein/Blum/Pelosi's. They have government paid staffers do the leg work. Pronto contract offers are hand delivered to the particular agency down the hall. Excuse me about the sequence. Maybe the valuable property that was chosen for dispersal was actually put into motion by Feinstein/Blum/Pelosi's. Now that's really evil.

In fact I think that's what happened when the World War II Naval installation at Treasure Island which is in San Francisco Bay and In San Francisco County was put on the block. That geography was well in control by Pelosi and Feinstein. Easy pickings. But a snag caught them. In their haste they didn't get an environmental report on the island before they signed the deal. Turns out Treasure Island is a toxic dump from WWII. Clean up by the superfund will cost millions and take more time than any one thought or planned. That project isn't going any where for a long while. With rising sea level it may never happen.

The Beatles in the 1960s wrote "Lady Madonna". It was a bouncy irreverent swipe at the Christian's Virgin Mary. The refrain goes "how does she manage to make ends meet?"

Estimates of Blum's income range as high as one hundred million per year. Remember when Dick with

Feinstein's help almost sold the Naval base at Long Beach to the Chinese some years back? Most people didn't know the deal was in the works despite the legal hurdles in getting the deal done. Blum would have received a huge commission through his real estate subsidiary. At the last minute the transaction made the papers and an outcry by everyone except co-California Senator Boxer stopped the sale. It appears Blum has an appropriate business subsidiary for whatever business he needs to deal with. I don't think he has an undertaker's certificate to operate. But if the draft starts up again he will be sure to have a booth at Arlington.

Over the years Senator Feinstein and Dick Blum have accumulated personal residential properties valued at approximately thirty-one million dollars. The properties include a Washington D.C. mansion, an Aspen, Colorado" ski chalet" and the latest is a sixteen million five hundred thousand mansion next to Gordon Getty's mansion in San Francisco. This last home alone has a yearly property tax of approximately one hundred and eighty thousand. Senator Feinstein's salary as a government representative is approximately one hundred and fifty thousand dollars per year. Well "how does she manage to make ends meet?" Hello Dickie Blum. He runs billion through his investment pools. Now those stakeholders either like Dickie's personality and competence or want access to Senator Feinstein. Here is a hint to the answer. He had no investment business of any note prior to hooking up with Di-Fi.

Conservative hawks in Washington are the same as progressive doves in Washington when it comes to stealing and abuse of power. To wit. Fifteen or so years ago then Secretary Of Defense Donald Rumsfeld under President George W. Bush wanted to close or downsize eight hundred military bases in fifty states. He says this will save two and one half billion dollars per year. That is an insignificant amount when one looks at the FY 2006 Defense budget of six hundred billion. The "saving" is less than one half of one percent. Iraq and Afghanistan then cost over six billion in one month. Communities around the nation would lose a significant amount of business when the bases are shuddered. The military payroll alone will be reduced by twenty-six thousand people. The private business's that serve those bases will suffer exponentially and will have to downsize also. In Keynesian terms, all those bases were net winners for local communities and the federal tax roles. The so-called savings turns out to be a loser in the bigger picture. It's all about context. Suppose Rumsfeld had another reason for closing bases in the United States. And the reason is to sell valuable government property to cronies at less than valuable prices.

Vice President Dick Cheney was the former CEO of Halliburton. Cheney was still a major shareholder in Halliburton. Halliburton was a large recipient of government contracts to service overseas base for the United States. Simple isn't it? Some added background about Cheney and Halliburton includes Cheney lobbying then President Clinton to get involved in the European stalemate with the Serbs and their conflict with the Muslims. Clinton jumped at the opportunity to get his name and Monica Lewinsky off the front page. Long story short American bombing runs in Serbia peaked at thirty-seven thousand in one day! Serbia eventually surrendered. The American public yawned at Clinton's escapade into Serbia. Cheney noticed and then cofounded the Project For The New American Century and it's goal of nation-building. We know how that turned out.

The problem for the tax payers is that both conservative and progressive thieves are in proximity to each other in Washington. It's like Butch Cassidy and the Sundance Kid and their Hole In The Wall Gang. The object of the Hole in the Wall Gang is diverting some of the federal governments trillions per year in tax receipts and in spending those funds. And the leakage is to be had by directing those contracts sometimes here sometimes there to the likes of Blum or to Pelosi or to Rumsfeld's cronies. No politician really calls time on other politicians for that abuse of power or constructively stealing from the tax payer because they all do it.

Time to plug the hole. Stop the flow of money and power to Washington and leave it in the states. More states rights. It's easier to watch and control a local thief than try to control and watch two—one at state level and one at federal level. We know where the local state officials live. And it's closer.

Of course local politicians should be watched carefully. But they are closer and you know where they live. Politicians and stealing go together. Here is a classic San Francisco progressive maneuver. Hiding larceny and bad judgment in a caring platitude ".as long as one person's life is saved, it's worth all the money we spend..."

The Golden Gate Bridge Board of Directors spent two million dollars to fund a study of adding a suicide barrier. Estimates of the barrier cost are about two hundred million dollars. Why do we need one? The Bridge opened in nineteen thirty-seven. Since then twelve hundred people jumped to their death. The past eighty three years show an average of fifteen deaths per year. Let's assume that history repeats itself. So over the next eighty-three years approximately another twelve hundred people choose to jump from the Bridge. If the cost is two hundred million then the prevention costs will be one hundred and twenty-five thousand per person maybe saved. Too much. Way too much money and it will not stop a determined suicide. There are too many other ways of ending one's life. Directors should take note, that the two million dollars spent on the study omits a fact. The fact is assisted suicide actually is legal as per the U.S. Supreme Court in the U.S. and in Oregon now. Also it can be done for under four thousand dollars.

California Senator Tom Ammiano who was the

instigator of the project while he was on the San Francisco Board of Supervisors also was on the Golden Gate Bridge Board. Self dealing and abuse of power no doubt in my mind. At the time he said, "This is a significant gesture that will be appreciated by the families affected."

So it's a two million dollar gesture ? Somebody has to work. It's not a gesture for the persons who actually work for the two million. The "affected families" won't get their family members back nor do I think that they stay awake at night thinking about prevention for some unknown next death. Or maybe he's not an idiot and will receive some contributions from the consultant group that is doing the study. So then he's not an idiot but only a simple thief. An assisted suicide can be had for under four thousand dollars. Stepping off a curb into the path of a bus is free. Spending one hundred and twenty-five thousand in a preemptive suicide prevention doesn't make sense. Particularly when the suicide knows best what's good for him/her.

One thing about Tom Ammano that I recall that was insightful. During Newsom's tenure as Mayor of San Francisco, Ammano was on the Board Of Supervisors. During an interview at that time by the local media Newsom's name came up concerning some difference of opinion between Ammino and Newson. Amman response included "... Gavin has two mommies ... Pelosi and Feinstein..." I believe that also.

P.S. During the retro fitting of the Bridge for a suicide prevention net located twenty feet below the pedestrian path on the bridge, a loud eerie hum has started during windy days. Looks like the threshold for the foreboding musical response is approximately thirty miles per hour. On very gusty days the "hum" can be heard three miles away. A spokesmen for the Bridge Authority blames rail enhancements to make the Bridge "safe". It looks like mission- creep in relation to the suicide prevention net has moved on to include bridge safety issues. Do vibrations and bridge safety go together? Don't think so. But the spokesman said they are going to fix it. Are we headed to a completely safe bridge by not having a bridge? Another progressive euphemism in essence is no bridge is a safe bridge. Looks like the progressives are backing into that solution. It's a money making solution for some one rather than a dubious construction safety solution. The prevention net is do to be completed in 2021. It's already over budget. Could the"hum" of the Bridge be a kind of "whistle blowing" of a government boondoggle ?

P.P.S.

"To be or not to be...", starts the soliloquy from Hamlet.

But the public doesn't know the reasons of the jumpers. Since the public is paying, they have the right to know what personal decisions of the jumpers they are interfering with. Maybe suicide is a reasonable and appropriate response to the jumpers problems. Maybe if the public knew what these jumpers were avoiding in real life they would have assisted the jumpers. With insufficient knowledge why prevent Golden Gate Bridge suicides? It's too late for philosophy or motivation reasons. The suicide net will be built. But saying nothing about things that are troubling is a bad habit to get into.

The other day while driving on Bush St near Grant Avenue in San Francisco an interesting entertainment occurred. Bush St there is fairly steep. It's also a crowded street of cars and many people in crosswalks. So I'm driving about twenty-five mph. A skateboarder passes me! He is swerving from lane to lane as to mitigate his speed. There are no brakes on skateboards. While swerving he's filming with a hand held iPhone. His brain darting from photo taking and navigating the streets ambient traffic along with controlling his speed invites my speculation when he will fall. This is San Francisco and has more attorneys in the Yellow Pages than anything else certainly individually and many other categories combined. I don't want to run over him. Because he is certainly worth more dead to his surviving relatives and acquaintances than alive. To slow his speed to a stop with a fast approaching crowded intersection he must slow down dramatically. To this purpose he lurches his skate board to the left at an almost forty-five degree angle. And then back to the right at a similar steep perpendicular angle. He's about 5'8" and weighs app 170 pounds. So the effective weight as per weight multiplied by speed is considerable. Particularly when the skate underpinnings weren't meant for such torque on a crumbly pavement. But he made it. Just in time to exit the street via a handicap ramp in place on the sidewalk. Could be ominously prophetic.

While we are down town, San Francisco's tall buildings do not have windows that open. One of the city's most attractive benefits is it's fresh air from the perpetual westerly. Yet the windows are permanently closed. The reason? The building is cheaper to build. Also a closed window building is less expensive to ventilate and heat.

Counterintuitively the buildings are built on unstable landfill that are themselves made up of the debris of former perpetual earthquakes. Why would they build such?Because more profit is to be had by economies of scale when building— tall buildings are more profitable. But the taller the building the less stable they become because of the bad leverage caused by the trembling structure.

So San Francisco builders have opted to rely on San Francisco's faults and at the same time it shut out it's strengths.

Last November 2019 was election time in San Francisco. What do Tim Cook of Apple, Mark Benioff of Salesforce and George Soros of doubtful character have in common besides being super wealthy? They and others support housing the homeless in

San Francisco. To that end they aggressively support propositions that fund at the tax payers expense free housing to any from any where who qualify. They are funding a proposition. They are not personally contributing to house and feed the homeless. Can it get any more disingenuous ? Of the three Benioff is the only one who actually lives in San Francisco. He lives three blocks from me in Presidio Heights.

How do you qualify to live on the streets in San Francisco? First, just show up and stake a claim so to speak on a sidewalk. Recently it was discovered that some other American cities were treating their own street sleepers to transportation to S.F. Second, be filthy so to be convincing. The major problem with caring for the homeless is quite another thing. Adopting the homeless is a budget buster for governments. And it doesn't solve the homeless problem It actually subsidizes homelessness. Maintenance is far more expensive and the ultimate costs are largely unknown when providing services to people who don't really care about themselves. These homeless caring billionaires should prove their sincerity by adopting street people themselves. Put them in the will? Have them over for dinner? Why should any government pay for a personal wish from a billionaire who could fulfill the wish personally?

Speaking of George Soros, he let it be known this past year that he has funded his Open Society Foundation with his net worth of $18 billion. Open Society Foundation's charter reads like a to do list for progressives. But many say his social equilibrium projects has a constructively illegal and subversive agenda. Recently the riots orchestrated by Black Lives Matter across the country has raised speculation that there is a connection to Open Society. Oakland's riots and traffic blocks on our Bay Bridge point to Black Lives Matter involvement and OSF funding. He's actually being sued by a Texas couple for their loss of a family member. The family member died in a riot that the parents said Soros Open Society Foundation instigated.

Suppose the Mafia tried to fund a philanthropic foundation with illegal profits. Don't think that would happen. But Soros is funding a foundation with legal funds that constructively supports and instigates subversive illegal actions. Its the mirror image of the Mafia hypothetical scheme. Soros spelled backwards is still Soros. His name is duplicity. By the way, of course Black Lives Matter but not as much if they are resisting arrest. Resisting arrest is a felony and is the foundation of all our criminal laws.

San Francisco homeless problem is in a crisis stage. Districts are variously infected. The main areas are in the commercial sections. Surrounded business operators who are losing business don't have the clouts or votes of primarily residential sections. Consequently the civil rights of defecating and urinating homeless is respected more than the shopping public and the shop owners who are exposed to these health hazards. In San Francisco, odd interpretations of Civil Rights Laws are in practice more important than the Health Code Laws.

Maybe it's because San Francisco is the place where same sex marriages began and their own special health hazards of HIV/AIDS. The foul living habits of the homeless is now folded in and becomes the new normal. It's OK. If AIDS/HIV is tolerated and supported by the Civil Rights Act then it follows we owe it to the homeless for free roaming filth production. Fact is HIV/AIDS kills more people now and has been doing so long before our bad flu season of Covid-19 ever showed up. Ebola Virus is a form of HIV/AIDS and Covid-19.

Progressives run San Francisco. If they wanted to stop filth on the streets they could. Simply get a determination that cholera or some such other diseases can suddenly occur because of these unchecked homeless conditions. But maybe the progressives with the prodding by Hollywood are using the homeless as a foil against anyone looking to shut down homosexual rights in the United States. Covid-19 and Ebola and HIV/AIDS are arguments for hygiene. Bacteria isn't politically correct. The ink is hardly dry on the Civil Rights Act and nature weighs in with her opinion on disease nurturing conditions with a quasi bacteria grenade thrown into the progressives street people's tent.

Chapter VI
Movie Reviews

I was meeting Bernie to get some background for a story idea that occurred to me because of events that happened last week in a Supreme Court judgment. Bernie is Jewish. I like Bernie. He speaks the Hollywood language of the Jews in that La La Land neighborhood. Like deceased Lew Washerman who was CEO of Music Corporation Of America (MCA) said to his Jewish colleagues, "Dress British, but think Yiddish".

A motion picture title that sums up Hollywood is "The Good, The Bad And The Ugly". Clint Eastwood starred in that film. He could have been all three subjects given his usual acting skill. What skill? Couldn't tell the difference between the three. He's very handsome and has a statuesque presence. That's it. He relies on that visage from any angle to carry him through from the start of the film to the conclusion. Conservative style to a fault in my view.

He's kind of like Greta Garbo's acting style. She is also more about her dramatic looks and her statuesque body contours. Greta and Clint costarring would have flopped. Because there would have been no movement in the movie. Questionable flammable ingredients with no spark.

I am a fan of certain Hollywood eras. Film noir, John Ford westerns plus his "Quiet Man". Stanley Kubrick's "Paths Of Glory" and his "Dr. Strangelove". Particularly I enjoyed the musicals. Fred Astaire and Ginger Rogers series. And that one with Fred Astaire and Eleanor Powell and Cole Porter music "Broadway Melody Of 1940". Both Eleanor And Fred in top form. Fred Astaire and Cyd Charisse in "The Band Wagon".

But modern films I have largely walked out on. Largely because of the F—- word. One comes to mind as the worst example of overused F— word coupled with sloppy and degenerative human behavior.

It covered a Wall Street panorama of lack of judgment motivated by criminal minds. The movie was "The Money Monster". I have financial markets experience. I wondered if the story and director in this edition of Hollywood and Wall Street was as good as Oliver Stone did in his movie "Wall Street "with perfectly cast Michael Douglas. It didn't happen. So I walked out.

This Hollywood treatment of a Wall Street scandal and indigenous characters was devalued of entertainment value for me because of the constant use of the

F...word. George Clooney headed up the Jodie Foster directed film. Actually Clooney opened the picture in a bathroom. Charming? He's talking through the bathroom door to a dilapidated Julia Roberts. From the start to fifteen minutes later when I threw in the towel the F.. word was in constant use. What is it about the F...word that present day Hollywood writers resort to its use gratuitously ? Well, It pads the script. A writer can count on the countless use of the F..word to fill out the dialogue.

All time Oscar winner for directing John Ford said acting "was in the eyes".That's where credibility in acting comes from. Maybe when one can't act they substitute expletives for dramatic effect. Bathroom scenes are another standard for placement in modern movies. I wonder why? Do real life Hollywood soirees include following guests to the restroom to keep continuity in the conversation? Maybe when screen writers combine the F...word with bathroom scenes, vomiting and gratuitous sex it adds up to sign language. Our schools don't teach critical and nuanced thinking. So vulgar sign language at a ultra low level is sure to make contact with the average audience that pay to see these kinds of Hollywood movies. SpencerTracy came up with his take on defining good acting'...don't let them catch you acting...'. Similar to what Ford said. It's about credibility.

Hollywood movies will probably stagnate at this low level given the political goals of inclusion in public schools rather than practical learning goals and an appreciation of the classic life. With an optimistic view maybe we have reached an inflection point and things may improve. Condescension gets old. One doesn't have to be bright to balk at yet another issue of injustice from days long gone bye be acknowledged and discussed and compensation formulated. Has the human run out of worthwhile goals? People are now only good for the caring they can offer if you listen to what the progressives preach. ? What kind of individuals does that breed? Increasingly Ivy League Schools have adopted an anti-elitism philosophy. Elitism? What is the definition of elitism? Is there only one? Or does defining elitism become like a scrum in rugby? Just get the ball any way you can and run with the ball until another definition eclipses the old definition. Which in some cases is only twenty-four hours old. But the new definition promises more guilt be extracted along with more compensation. Anti-elitism as practiced by the progressives is in essence anti - meritocracy and care giving being substituted. That's no future. That's like going through garbage cans. Care giving has its place. But it should not be recommended as a national goal.

Chapter VII
Homeless

A person called a philosopher was centuries ago a high honor. Well now if a person is called a rockstar that is the ultimate. Philosopher being replaced by rockstar speaks volumes about the evolution or the devolution of our society.

The last time I saw a rockstar, he was emaciated and raging. He couldn't speak clearly or quietly and looked like he needed a shower with the strongest cleaning solvents allowed on human skin.

On the other hand my last experience with a philosopher was reading Plato's twenty-five hundred year old accounts of Socratic conversations. Something entirely different. They did share one common thread. Both the philosopher Socrates and the rockstar indulged in a kind of rage. Both commented on society. But the rockstar's rage was brutal, blurred and hard to follow. The philosopher's rage was thoughtful and pleasant.

History and nature has supported the fact that hygiene is more important than individuals rights. No hygiene then no history. Count on it. Cholera will insure a civilization wont last a generation. And importantly, property rights are more important than individual rights. Take some ones property illegally is like killing some one. Progressives can't tolerate any law that preempts individual rights. Progressives need a short cut to success to attract voters. The short cut is preemptively devaluing actual talent and hard work and constructively stealing property so members of their political party look more equal. Basically pro- gressives follow a glacial- speed- moving -quasi- chip -away-pilfering-thieving-now-you-see-it-now-you- don't- philosophy-of-wealth-distribution.

Progressives use the Civil Rights Act in place of the Constitution. Four and one half billion years of evolution via natural law led to one hundred and seventy-three years of Constitutional law which led to fifty-six years of Civil Rights Law. At the same time our laws are getting more at odds with natural law, the world's population is approaching eight billion. How will the eight be housed and fed? How will the children of the eight be housed and fed? The slow motion train wreck of presumptuous laws which promise equality and which are necessarily more costly are sounding loud train whistles.

Now in San Francisco no body talks about the health code. They talk more about individual rights. In the Summer Of Love the flower children didn't smell fresh. I was there and I was a witness—-at a distance. Many slept in doorways or overcrowded lodgings. Consequently the bugs thrived on the decaying atmosphere.

No one has the right to contaminate the public areas. Sidewalks don't flush. Urban renewal is more important than the homeless. The 8th Amendment barring of "cruel and unusual punishment" has nothing to do with clearing public walkways of sleeping bums.

Who would deny these statements? Judge Kim McLane Wardlaw does. She sits on the U.S. Court of Appeals for the 9th Circuit in San Francisco. She was recommended to the court by a former hippy President Clinton in 2006. He referred to the fact that she has some Hispanic heritage as one of his reasons for her nomination. An example of identity politics in full view. How idiotic. That's hippy logic that has lasted and thrived and become caricature.

In 2006 she ruled in the majority of a 2-1 panel that invalidated a 37 year old ordinance in Los Angeles. She wrote in her opinion, "The 8th Amendment barring 'cruel and unusual punishment' prohibits Los Angeles from punishing involuntary sitting, lying or sleeping on public sidewalks that is an unavoidable consequence of being human and homeless without shelter." She is a moron.

The area in question in L.A. is 50 blocks square. It is called Skid Row. Recently there has been an urban renewal of part of that area. New apartments and con-dominiums have been built. That's good for the city and it's people. But the new inhabitants resent that homeless have to be stepped over or avoided because they might be dangerous. Enter the Los Angeles Police Department to clear the area. Then enter activ-ist lawyers that are pro homeless on a pro bono basis but are paid by our government and ultimately by tax payers. Then enter Judge Wardlaw.

One wonders about Judge Wardlaw's personal hygiene habits when she ignores the descriptions of what the downside is of sidewalks that don't flush. But one shouldn't wonder that she is incompetent and should be removed from the bench. Again. No one has the liberty or right to contaminate public areas. And this was the seminal ruling that allowed the homeless to stop paying rent and start living free on the streets.

Here in San Francisco they come from all over to take advantage of the moderate climate and the keys to the city so to speak. I saw two "homeless"white young men interviewed by the local news. One was thirty-two and the other was thirty-six. When asked why they came to San Francisco [without flowers in their hair] They both replied that "they wanted to meet new people".

San Francisco is in a panic about Covid-19 but at the same time has more than accommodated filthy sidewalk sleepers who are disease carriers. Here is the caricature of individual rights trumping public property laws and trumping health code laws. Why do San Franciscan's warmly tolerate HIV/AIDS which kills more than Covid-19? In a word —Hollywood.

So the Summer Of Love hippies influenced then hippy and now former President Bill Clinton to appoint a daughter of a hippy who was part Hispanic. She is Judge Kim Mc Clane Wardlaw who ruled that the Summer Of Love hippy sleeping arrangements without regard to hygiene is now the law of the land.

Chapter VIII
What They Teach In Schools

The original contributors of the endowments to the eight Ivy League Schools are long gone. The eight schools are: Brown, Harvard, Cornell, Princeton, Dartmouth, Yale, Columbia and University Of Pennsylvania. The heirs never earned the billions so now they give it away without strings attached. So easy come easy go. The students will have to learn the hard way about critical thinking if they are not instructed at the universities. They will have to learn survival instincts before it's too late.

Two-hundred and sixty-nine year old Princeton University recently announced a settlement with an upstart social justice group less than a year old. It's name is The Black Justice League. The group petitioned the president of the university about removing President Woodrow Wilson's (1913-1921) name from the campus. This includes the Woodrow Wilson School of Public And International Affairs. A thirty-two hour sit-in ended at the President of Princeton

Office President Christopher Eisgruber. He will hear the group about it's petition and try to find a way forward. The Black Justice League thinks Woodrow Wilson was a racist because he supported segregation. Segregation was legal at the time of Wilson's presidency. It was illegal after the Civil Rights Act of 1964. Segregation according to capability has its place in schooling. Why hold back smarter children? Why make less smart children feel embarrassed?

So along come affirmative action Black Justice League students. They leaned into a positive curriculum of valuable learning. Rather they distracted the student body with a nihilistic adventure. Maybe the Black Justice League couldn't make the grade. So distract others on the campus who can make the grade. Taking Woodrow Wilson's name off public buildings is a definite revision of history. Suppose historians redacted Adolph Hitler from history books?The lessen of Hitler's policies in retrospect would invite a horrific repeat in real time to learn all over again about that historic evil.

Contemporaneously, just north of Princeton in Rhode Island, Brown University's Committee On Slavery made public it's recommendations to the school's president. The recommendations included, "The construction of a memorial, starting up a center for slavery studies, increasing efforts to recruit foreigners, particularly from Africa and the West Indies. Also Brown should publicly and persistently acknowledge it's slave ties particularly in freshman orientation".

The Committee was formed 3 years ago under the direction of the first black Ivy League School's president, Ruth J. Simmons. She is the great-grand-daughter of a slave. She is also a probable example of affirmative action and what can go wrong with affirmative action. Also President Simmons is taking her history out of context. It's well known that slaves bought and brought from Africa by white slavers actually bought the slaves from tribal chiefs and/or family members in Africa. Both buyer and sellers of black slaves thought they were getting value with the transaction.

Why is Brown looking backwards on issues that aren't timely or important? Slavery at the time was legal. It doesn't make it morally acceptable but to spend valuable and expensive time on non-critical education issues is a luxury and is very negative. How do Simmons and the Committee reconcile their pre-occupation with 17th century slavery and it's negative connotations with their push for more African and West Indies students to come to America and Brown in particular if America's roots are so bad and can-not be forgotten or erased ?Of course it's better not to ask tough questions to people who got their jobs not based on merit. As President of Brown University Ruth Simmons earns approximately $ 676,000 per year. That does not include perks. What was she deprived of had she still lived in West Africa? Fact is slavery exists in Africa today.

On the other hand, what has America gained or lost from Simmons' ancestors coming to our shores? Important anecdotal facts regarding that question can be summed up by some statistics from Centers For Disease Control. The highest rate of suicides per 100,000 in the United States are the American Indian males and the Alaskan Native males—-Eskimos. They tally 27.61 per 100K. They are followed closely by white males at 25.96 per 100K. The lowest rate of suicides per 100,000 of ANY RACE are black females at 6.71 per 100K. That would include President Ruth Simmons category.

Something is terribly wrong. When the original American Indian warriors and their sea faring counterpart the Eskimos collectively commit more suicides in modern day America than black women who are prone to be statistically over weight and complaining civil rights junkies. And one of these black females heads up a heretofore prestigious university. And her focus is slave issues. Is that helpful to some one seeking employment? Simmons does practice selling guilt which has no known commercial value. President Ruth Simmons is a Marxist Leninist. She doesn't teach. She destroys. Simmons and the progressives are always rummaging through the garbage cans of history. Picking out rotten and decaying truths, half truths and lies. All of the rot is out of the context of the era and the packaging of circumstances. Then Simmons wants to sell this stink for guilt money.

Ironically the white male has also suffered a like

fate of the original American indigenous peoples. For the part he played in prosecuting a slow motion genocide of native Americans and bringing blacks from Africa and mistakenly creating The Civil Rights Act Of 1964 to make them feel comfy. He now suffers the scourge of political correctness lashes on a legal collective punishment reservation. A more equitable suicide rate would be arrived at by a repeal of the Civil Rights Act of 1964. People who want to take their own lives should not have the law as a reason.

Chapter IX
Mike's
Memories

Where's Bernie? I better check my watch. I'm still early. Do I need a martini? Nah. Start at the same time. Talking is about communication and nuances. Liquor can spoil both. I need to check with Bernie. I want to know whether he has heard anything too support my suspicions that the LGBTQ+ members are on the threshold of a monumental project of launching a new race aided by the science of gene-editing? And all those royalties from patented genomes that go along with the newbies. Or am I wrong? It would be a great story. But to have legs and sell books it has to be true. Or circumstantially close to true. Bernie could have the answers. I have evidence to support my suspicions.

I asked him once, "Is there any subject that Hollywood wont touch?"

Bernie answered," Nothing is sacred. The public will watch and believe anything. You know how I know?"

"Please tell me Bernie."

Bernie replies, "Two thousand years ago a hippy Jew named Jesus said he was the son of god. And audiences still go to the theater to see stories of Jesus when there not in church praying to him."

Chuckling, I responded "Gotcha."

There's Alioto's. It's next to Fishermen's Grotto Restaurant. The Grotto also dates back to the 1920's. It still is owned and operated by the Geraldi Family. Larry Geraldi was a neighbor of mine in Woodside. I lived in Woodside from 1978 to 1988. We had horses on the property —-five acres. Woodside was and still is a horse community. It has dedicated horse riding trails dating back to the 1930's. The Woodside Trail Club still exists and my wife and I are still members. We have keys issued by the club to ride on private easements. Some of those dedicated easements have been in place for almost one hundred years. We have two horses. They were our show horses. But now they are personal riding horses. We did compete nationally with our Morgan Horses for many years. We did well.

One of the original founders of the trail club was Lurline Matson. She was the heiress of the Matson Shipping Line. Also I believe the daughter of A.P. Gianinni, who was founder of Bank Of America, was an original founder and member of The Woodside Trail Club. I know where her property was when she lived in Woodside. She called it "Champagne Stables". She raised and showed world class Saddlebred horses.

Woodside is contiguous to other horse back riding lands. Inclusive of Stanford lands where the Stanford Linear Accelerator is today. On that land is also the "monkey trail" which is so named because of advanced primate studies are held there. That's close to Searsville Lake—lovely land. There is also some San Francisco Water Department watershed and Wunderlich and Huddart Parks with trails the lead over Skyline and onto the beaches if you really feel adventurous. All added up it is thirty-seven thousand acres of a mixed forested wonderland. And it's in the middle of this heavily populated Bay Area.

Quite a treat. We sold our property in nineteen eighty-eight to John Sculley of Apple Computer. We bought the property in nineteen seventy-eight. It was five acres on a flag lot which was private and quiet. After ten years and ten to fifteen thousand dollars per month upkeep it gets old. Particularly when I'm playing the markets for my daily bread and for my horses daily alfalfa. Even Hercules had to sit down. Looking back we lived at the property longer than the Sculleys and longer than the Stauffer Chemical heiress who we bought the property from.

Sculley sold the property to some one who didn't live there as long as John and his wife. The only person who lived on my former property longer than us was the original owner. He had apple orchards there on a commercial scale. For myself and my wife the property was a special place for us and our horses. That's why we prevailed and got the most enjoyment and satisfaction from the property. Do things for your passions. It's better than working just for money.

After the sale we moved our stock to Larry Geraldi's just down the road. He used to race horses nationally and did well. He left Fisherman's Grotto as a young man in his twenties. He borrowed the seed money from his older brother. Larry was an impulsive type. He didn't like to be part of a team particularly if they were his family. He opened The Domino Club in downtown San Francisco. The name of the club was accurate. Diners at the club were offered a set of dominos and score board if they wished. Money was bet. Drinks came with the food which was tasty. It was on Trinity Street. It was one block long near Bush and Montgomery Street.

It was quite a watering hole. Like Toots Schorr's in New York but not on that scale. He like to tell me stories about the Domino Club. He was a little older than me. And I liked to hear about celebrities who regularly stopped into the club when in town. He could have written a gossip column. But the celebrities would have stopped coming in if Larry spread stories about their private activities. Bad for business. No column just food and drinks worked better. He spoke in a stream of consciousness. Plucking memories randomly.

For instance he remarked how dramatically good looking Rick Nelson was. Only in person could his features be appreciated. They said that about Ava

Gardner also. Rick needed help with a professional sex contact. Larry could help. Rick knew he could help. That's why Rick was there.

At another time Burt Lancaster was interested in the same menu choice. Larry suggested Carol Doda to Burt also. Larry made arrangements. No charge. Larry said both men preferred oral sex according to Doda. She also said Lancaster was always in a rush. Larry made reference to "a la carte choice" . I don't know what her performance fee was. I didn't ask. I found the best way to be entertained by Larry was just let him go. Let him talk without disruption. He liked that. I knew he did.

Doda was one of the first topless dancers in San Francisco. She also was the first I had seen who used silicone enhancements. I didn't like that. Her breasts became cartoons. Nothing like the real thing. Even if what's real isn't much. She also was a successful club operator on Broadway Street in the north beach area of San Francisco.

There was Nat King Cole who liked getting together with local stripper Tempest Storm. Cole came in quite often to sing at the Venetian Room in the Fairmont Hotel atop Nob Hill. I saw him there. He was excellent. Hard worker. Never took his audience for granted. He gave them a memorable performance every time.

I also caught Ella Fitzgerald at the same venue. She worked as hard as Sinatra. She was completely original. Her choice of music reflected her intelligence. It's fine to have a talented voice. But to excel and to be remembered require the right song and the right arrangement. Of all components I think the arrangement is the most important. For me Nelson Riddle and his orchestra was the best arranger of music in the twentieth century. Riddle and his orchestra worked at Capitol Records. He worked with Sinatra, Fitzgerald, Dean Martin, Nat King Cole, Judy Garland, Peggy Lee, Johnny Mathis, Rosemary Clooney, Keely Smith, next generation rock singer Linda Ronstadt and opera singer Kiri Takanawa and others. For me Riddle got the most out of those singers. He was an explosion of creative sound blending among diverse musical instruments. A brain like Riddles could do many things but I'm happy to witness his musical applications.

My favorite restaurant was Alexis' Tangier. It was in San Francisco. Lucky me. It was across the street from The Fairmont. It was in business from 1950-early 1970's. I found out about it late. It was on two floors. The ground floor had the restaurant. I usually ordered the rack of lamb. My dates enjoyed the rack and sometimes pheasant under glass. Any thing on the menu worked. After dinner, steps led downstairs to the Gypsy Room. It had a pianist and a roving violin player. They took requests. The drinks were excellent. At that time I drank Courvoisier V.S.O.P. cognac. Can't drink it now. Too strong. On the same floor behind two-foot thick doors was a discotheque with a excellent dance floor and tables arranged around. Very good choice of recorded rock music. The capacity was maybe one hundred people. But it was still cozy and charming despite maxed attendance . The decor was high quality in a middle eastern theme. The gals with their dates were super and all knew how to dress and could afford high end duds—-super. Usually between dinner, drinks and dancing all added up it would be four to five hours at Alexis' Tangier. What a ball.

Some of Geraldi's trivia that remains with me included one of my favorite actresses Jean Simmons. She was great in Elmer Gantry and The Big Country. Larry said she had rather large thighs and legs. And she liked her drinks. Charming and intelligent woman according to Geraldi. Meryl Streep was in once. Spencer Tracy once said, "Don't let them catch you acting." She won the Academy Award for Best Actress in the motion picture "The Iron Lady". I saw the film. Streep didn't follow Tracy's caveat. She so mimicked Lady Margaret Thatcher that the "Iron Lady" rose from her grave and was on screen. Streep could have won a "Graphic Animation Award for Special Effects Performed by a Human" if there was such a category. Meryl Streep was spooky. That indeed was great acting. But it was without warmth.

San Francisco is a place many motion pictures are filmed. The set and background are free and singularly spectacular. Frank Sinatra was in town shooting a film. Maybe it was Pal Joey with Rita Hayworth and Kim Novak. One day Sinatra was inside a actors personal movie trailer out front of the Domino Club. One of the grips of the film mentioned it to Larry while he was making drinks. Larry jumped at the chance to meet Frank. He goes into the trailer. Sinatra says "Hi" ———almost no eye contact with Larry according to Giraldi. Frank didn't stand up or extend his hand for a shake or make Larry comfortable. So Larry being a proud Sicilian says nothing turns around and leaves. Oh yeah, that's Larry.

Then the stories about former United States Senator Barbara Boxer. She was a frequent attendee at the Domino club. Particularly when the crew from ABC NEWS were in attendance. She had an idea for a TV show. It would be called "Boxer Shorts". I'm not kidding. She was aggressive and had a sexual appetite. She never had a ride home. I went to school with a guy who in fact did take her home late one night from the Domino Club. Her husband Stewart was upstairs. It was very late. That didn't stop them. Just show up. Anything can happen in life. Ask my friend. Actually he passed away some time ago. Ask Boxer if she thinks her qualifications or her persistence was the reason for successful politics.

Most every car in the parking lot of Alioto's shows the results of casual carpet-bombing by the local sea gulls. It's like forensic evidence. A sleuth could roughly determine how long a car has been in the parking lot by the amount of bird dropped clues. Street level entrance to the restaurant is situated behind fishmongers and boiling crab pots. They are always busy in some degree. Alioto's restaurant level is up two flights of stairs. Each flight including the walls and landings display fifty to eighty year old photos of prior generations of the Alioto clan greeting customers or just smiling for a group photo by a camera that is ancient compared todays iPhone editions. And all those people in the photos are akin to discovering cave art in France or elsewhere. The men wear suits with carefully knotted ties. The women who are full-bodied smile broadly. All are proud of their family's place of business. Straight forward attitude. Healthy looking. Faces that reflect hard work experience with a hint of philosophical attitude by the look in their eyes. In a word. Polite. Not antiseptic polite. Not condescending polite. But eager and offering professional help to the customer who could be a friend after the business was done. There is an elevator. But no photos in the elevator. Some what like our own modern experience of travel. The ride is quicker. But one misses out on the trip.

Chapter X
Alioto's
And Bay
Environment

I made it. I'm early.

"Hi Mr. Genoa". It was the familiar voice of Alioto host, Marty.

"Hey Marty ... how ya been?"

"I have no complaints ... getting older ... but aren't we all."

"Just think Marty, the Rolling Stones are our age...people don't go to their concerts to observe four old guys ... they go for the performance ... keep performing".

"I'm so glad you came in ... how many today?"

" I'm early ... there will be one more ... his name is Bernie Glow ... can I have a table by the window?"

"You bet...follow me."

Marty led to a table which had a marina view. I

could have been in the crows nest of one of the fishing boats.

"I heard Fat Joey died."

"Yeah about a year ago ... Joe junior now runs the restaurant ... when he comes in I'll tell him your are here."

"Every time any one says "Joe" at Alioto's half the floor turns their heads."

"I know what you mean ... that's Italian....we call Fat Joeys son Junior to stop the confusion ... would you like a drink and something to nibble on?"

"No Marty ... I'll wait for my friend to arrive ... maybe fifteen or thirty minutes".

"OK ... let me know if you change your mind ... I'll bring a glass of water".

"Anything special on the menu?"

"Yeah ... "Veggies A La Fat Joey" ... kind'a honorary menu choice in his memory"

"Veggies A La Fat Joey?" That's an oxymoron isn't it?"

"It's Italian ... enjoy the lunch".

Could be a half hour till Bernie is do. The second story panorama of the marina filled with fishing boats spreads out before me. Most of the fishing boats were built seventy or eighty years ago. Some maybe 90 years old. I think they were built by the fishermen themselves. They built the boats. Then they used the boats. They caught the fish. They harvested the crabs. Then they fed their families. And then they put the ocean harvest on a menu and served hungry tourists. From immigrant to boatwright to fisherman to maintainer of fishing tackle and chandler of boat maintenance to cooks, kitchen staff, waiters with eating recommendations and cleaning and closing up at midnight. Then do it again tomorrow. Starting very early.

No time for television. If there was TV offered. The radio was useful. A measure of escape delivered by Frank Sinatra, Dean Martin or Tony Bennet singing Cole Porter or Rodgers and Hart. Sinatra's mother was a legal secretary. I like to think that's where Frank got the articulate diction and his tireless work ethic. According to an interview I caught, Frank mentioned that his mother was a taskmaster. During the interview he went to a bird cage and checked on his and Barbara Marx Sinatra's parakeet. The birds name was Dolly. Frank's mother was nicknamed Dolly. The bird reacted to Frank's visit by opening his beak in a threatening manner. Sinatra remarks "You little shit. You have a personality like my mother. That's why you're named after my mother". Sinatra's work ethic and articulate voice delivery coupled with his personal creed to follow the intent of the composer's words provided a comforting trip from the radio to somewhere else at the time the trip home late at night was being endured by the worn out worker. Some of the older family members still preferred Caruso and operas and folk songs from Italy in the home language.

There's Alcatraz. It means pelican in the local Indian language. Where are the descendants of those Indians? I can't imagine what wildlife and wildfowl populated the Bay four hundred years ago when the Spanish and the Russians showed up. Tiburon which is due north across from where I'm sitting is the Spanish word for shark. I imagine that there must have been tens of thousand of seals and sea otters in the bay if the Spanish thought that land should be named after a predator. Seals were after fish and abalone and other crustaceans. Sea otters were also after the same diet, And the sharks were after the seals and the otters. Sounds familiar. Don't hear much about availability of abalone. Some seals. Some pelicans. But hardly any ducks or geese now. And the other predator who kills for pelts and not to live were the Russians along with Spanish. Man shows up. Everything else disappears proportionally. That's the real wrecking crew—the human. There are so many of we humans now that the living things we eat have a better pedigree than us.

There's a seal in the harbor. Time was seals and otters saturated the bay. Today there's one seal that I see. And I saw a small flock of pelicans earlier. Now I'm in a restaurant overlooking structurally unremarkable fishing boats that catch fish and crabs that live in polluted waters. Take Take Take. And we hardly clean up afterwards.

Man marches on. Before there were places like Africa all over the planet. Now settlements like China increasingly take their place. We in North America are in-between Africa and China results.

Some years ago the Yangtze River turned a bright red near an industrial city. It's not the first time. This has happened before. Officials suspect illegal dumping of chemicals. The river is the longest in Asia. It's the third longest in the world. The Yangtze basin supports half of China's crop production. River dolphins have gone extinct. Fish kills have multiplied.

There are about one billion four hundred million Chinese. There are only twelve hundred Pandas in the wild. Endangered animals, toxins and heavy metals have been found in Chinese medicines and food.

Now China mines in Africa. Now China logs in Africa.

The Yangtze and bacteria from the petri dish of one billion four hundred million Chinese have revenged humans frivolous behavior and delivered yet another pandemic—Covid-19— to China and the rest of the planet.

We in the United States have our own unique environmental wrecking crew. We are only approximately four percent of the worlds population but we are consumers of about twenty-five percent of the worlds out put. Interestingly recent Covid-19 statistics show the United States with twenty-five percent of the world's infections. Looks like nature is keeping score. If we consume twenty five percent of the worlds produce we are inviting a similar twenty five percent of disease that comes from over consumption. I think that's fair. I like to think the same way as the universe's metaphysic thinks and works.

For example, Blackstone Group LP raises money from wealthy individuals. It invests in most anything. Uganda has some of the last untouched jungles on the planet. Blackstone contacts Uganda's government and offers its services. I.E. We have money to invest, what do you want? Uganda says how about funding a dam project? We need electricity. We will donate the property. You arrange financing. When electricity flows we will pay you back with interest. Blackstone in far away New York nods yes and pushes some input keys on a computer. Voila! Out comes a fully detailed agreement. Work starts and the Ugandan jungle is partially demolished by huge earth moving equipment. Animals and fish are dislocated forever. Blackstone in far away New York through the alchemy of money has created wealth for partners at the expense of serenity and beauty in the African jungle. Recently Ebola reached U.S. shores. It's a kind of revenge by the planet for disturbing natures metaphysic of seeking real time balance.

The western backed help to African nations with antibiotics created over population on the African continent. Those alchemical people need food. That's how

Ebola crept into the population. The alchemical people ate mammals that they should not have—bats. Hence Ebola. Nature found out. Can't hide anything from nature. Hence nature sent out Ebola virus to right the ship so to speak. Another gambit by the planet in it's pursuit of balance.

Consider the collateral damage from all of the above to corn. Corn comes beautifully husked with elegant silk styles inside for protection and also provides a decorative flair. It was picked off stalks that could be 10 feet tall in the quiet fields of what were the Great Plains. Corn is stored sunlight with all the nutrients that it could absorb from the earth and the moisture of past rains. It provides nutritional food for a later time. That's where we started.

But now it has become a commodity that Goldman Sachs and other thieves and alchemists from Wall Street want to corner. They want to drive up the price so their managed accounts can have exorbitant profits. Some of those profits will help Goldman pay for its new forty three story building at 200 West Street in Manhattan. The construction costs are app. $2.4 billion. What was affordable corn now affords "Guys n' Dolls" dressed brokers inappropriate overpriced clothing.

Then there are the thieves in our Congress that want to use corn as a weapon against terrorists by mitigating the accumulation of petrodollars in the Mideast. Never mind that the corn-based ethanol costs more to produce than it can be sold for. The actual beneficiary of this boondoggle are the corn lobbys. How are you going to keep them down on the farm, once they know how to steal big time?

What's a body to do? Vote Libertarian, promote population REDUCTION and plant or share a garden.

How about the issues on the San Francisco ballots come voting season? It's almost like reading the funny papers. I remember in 2008. There was a peace initiative on the San Francisco ballot. It was Proposition C. It was the idea of Director Da Vid's Global Peace Foundation. It promised world peace by transforming Alcatraz Island. How would that happen and why would transformation bring peace? Hippys never have to explain. They only have to posture and yell. More yelling than posturing. The organization proposed building a hexagram structure in place of the prison. Then the structure will lead to a "deep meditative, transpersonal and transcendent experience". There's no money back guarantee that it will help make a more peaceful world. But if ya don't try ya don't get. Hey Da Vid, if that's your real name, Alcatraz Island is already peaceful. Why don't you and your "transpersonals" make a pilgrimage to war-torn Iraq because of our criminal invasion with the message you have. Better yet go to Washington and picket the Pentagon with your peace message.

Da Vid had tipped one card already. He's mentioned Bechtel Corp as a possible source of spade money to transform the under- exploited Island. "Under-exploited island"? Ask a family of Pelicans. Where there is Bechtel there is certainly the other money grubbers, Feinstein and operative hubby Dickie Blum, Walter Shorenstein who together want to sell tickets to other peoples property.

I got an idea. How about we just let the Pelicans and other birds use the Island for a peaceful sanctuary? I voted No On C. Others did also. The Prop failed. The pelicans are happy.

Speaking about wildfowl. Bring them back. According to the Bay Conservation And Development Commission, the coming predicted 3 feet rise in ocean waters will change the Bay Area landscape dramatically. Notably the three feet rise which is possible by the year 2100 is a median estimate. Some estimates range as high as a fifteen foot increase. Areas lost to the rising waters will vary according to elevation, from a few feet to miles or more.

And so the alchemy of filling in the bay for the past 100 years so that land and wealth could be created is turning into another foolhardy scheme. Mother nature has taken notice of the missing land. As has the wildfowl. Variations on this not-thought-through plan are increasingly being replicated around the globe today. Indonesia, Philippines, Bangladesh and others are recent examples of what clearing tree cover and building communities on flood plains or inappropriate sites produce in disasters.

The Bay Area has time to prepare. But dikes, sea walls, levees or berms are not the answer. They just kick the problem down stream. Think Hurricane Katrina and New Orleans. Less population and responsible conservation is the answer. The net effect of the coming inundation will give better situated Bay Area residents a second chance to see what the Bay looked like before real estate developers showed up. Personally I look forward to seeing more wildfowl.

Thinking about greedy people and other peoples money and property, the charity Oxfam published a jarring statistic two days ago. The top eight wealthiest people have assets equal to three and one half billion of the worlds poorest. So the bottom half according to Oxfam has approximately $430 billion in assets compared to a similar asset tote of the most wealthy. The progressives and other acronyms who are in the wealth distribution business immediately rubbed their collective hands in shock and an equal amount of glee. After all it's a fact that could equate into a massive amount of "charity"with other peoples money.

Hold on Oxfam. So what's to be done? Do you really want to take a significant amount of $430 billion and put into the hands of the worlds poorest? Those 3.6 billion people are poor largely because they shouldn't have been born in the first place. I know. It's sounds harsh. But do you really want the 3.6 billion to have more children and put more pressure on the environment?Here's a thought. Maybe the eight wealthiest buy the reproductive rights of the poorest 3.6 billion. That way the poor will enjoy a windfall And the planet will have some extra years.

I remember fitness guru Jack LaLanne swam from Fisherman's Wharf to Alcatraz in handcuffs when he was sixty years old in 1970. Jack also had an informal weight lifting contest against Arnold Schwarzenegger when Jack was fifty- four and Arnold was twenty-one. Jack beat Arnie. It was an unofficial contest. But Arnold called him ".an animal." Later when Schwarzenegger was elected Governor of California he put Jack on a state fitness committee and inducted LaLanne into California's Hall Of Fame.

To the left of Tiburon directly across the bay under the Golden Gate Bridge is Fort Baker. I did two weeks of active duty summer camp there when I was in the National Guard. I almost went to Viet Nam because I ducked out so many times. They call it AWOL (Absent Without Leave). I would be present for the morning attendance about six AM with the rest of the company. But then I disappeared. Usually I went into Tiburon or Sausalito and had a hearty breakfast which included a Ramos Fizz. The Corinthian Yacht Club made the best fizz. Then I would walk around the rest of the day in my uniform. Must have looked like a lost dog. I would show up back at the parade grounds for final head count about four PM. Did that for two weeks. Until it occurred to my Lieutenant who commanded my company that he never saw me between six AM and four PM. I was a file clerk. He never saw me in the office.

Because I never went to the office. But it was pointed out or he figured it out. He was furious. He called me to his office and challenged me for explanation of my whereabouts during during that time. I had no excuse. At that time, National Guard duty was a legal way to avoid the draft which meant that I maybe could get sent to Viet Nam. So he told me that he was going to charge me with being AWOL and boot me out of Californias National Guard. That would make me eligible for the draft and I was 4A which made me very likely for a ten thousand mile journey to Viet Nam so I could kill people I didn't know for reasons that made no sense. I needed a lawyer. My father had a well connected lawyer. His name was Steven Leonoudakis. His law partner was California Senator John Foran. Steve got on the phone to my company commander and persuaded the lieutenant that if I was drafted it would upset my mother dangerously because of her frail asthmatic condition. Which was true. Steve was very skillful. And I got a general discharge from The National Guard which didn't make me immediately liable for active duty in the regular army. Whew. That taught me a lesson in discipline that I have never forgotten.

During my National Guard experience I was called up twice for active duty in quelling California riots. Once called up for Watts riots in Los Angeles. The other call up was for riots in Berkeley. Both riots had to do with civil rights and antiwar grievances. Both times Governor Edmond "Pat" Brown was in charge.

He was the father of former governor Jerry Brown. Both times I and others in the guard were sent out in open bed trucks after curfew which was at six or eight PM. We were to maintain curfew enforcement among the African American natives who were burning down their own neighborhoods and looting as they went. Governor Brown didn't allow members of the Guard to have ammunition! We were sitting ducks. That's what most politicians think of people. They are just chess pieces that are always subject to being expendable when it's politically correct to do that trade. The heavy lifting of law enforcement was done by the Los Angeles Police Department. We just stood there in an intersection for example and pretended to be intimidating scenery with no bullets. The LAPD knew their stuff. Got a problem? Call them. They got bullets and they know where they want them to go.

Progressives like Governor Edmond "Pat" Brown and his son Jerry are consumed with "identity politics". That's why straight white males like me were expendable in Watts and Berkeley. The recent examples of statues of Southern generals being torn down and names of professional sports teams being forced to change their historic personas because of public intimidation is not new.

In nineteen seventy-two Stanford University dropped Indians as the name of it's team and retired the Indian team mascot. Fifty-five native Americans out of a general student body population of app. 15,000 used guilt to shame the mostly straight white males to turn in the name and mascot and constructively their testicles. They used The Civil Rights Acts Of 1964 as a tool of extortion. I.E. if there is any minority griev- ance that needs money or power or fixing just accuse straight white males of insensitivity. And voila! You will have the progressive press, descendants form the 19th century slave trade, unloved women and Irish politicians flex their vitriol to steam roll opposi- tion to capitulate.

And what did Stanford replace "Indians" with? The effete school leadership gathered all their criti- cal thinking ability to conjure "cardinal". Note, not even plural. Cardinal for color. Period. What the fuck does that mean? What the fuck kind of image is cardinal that a school can root for? All that higher education subverted to produce no passion for excel- lence. Instead we get care givers. Isn't that so 1960's? Interestingly, since the time of the mascot and name change, Stanford has lagged in mens sports and done better in women sports .No balls there.

In 1970 Stanford quarterback Jim Plunkett won the Heisman Trophy along with two other prestigious awards. He was part Indian. He was in fact an Indian and played for a team called the Indians. Homeric irony exposing identity politics as an empty gesture.

Chapter XI
Mike Meets Junior

"Hi Mister Genoa ... I'm Junior ... I don't think we have met ".

Junior was handsome. He reminded me of his grandfather Frank. Frank Alioto was a very successful restauranteur. Junior was in excellent shape maybe forty-five or fifty years old. He was not like Fat Joey his father. It occurred to me that maybe there was an inflection point in generational and more importantly cultural replacements away from the progressive paradigm. From snowflakes to no nonsense Italians. Pendulums can swing in one direction just so far.

I stood up. "Junior, so glad Marty told you I wanted to meet you ... no ... we have not met ... sorry about dad ... he was a classic ... lot of fun."

"I miss him Mister Genoa."

" Call me Mike, please ... how do stay so fit?"

" Swim, run and watch the diet ... and you?"

"I fence ... took it up late.. ... one of the best things I ever did...along with riding horses for thirty-four years ... please sit down ... how's business?"

"Business is great ... the mix of people is a blur ... from all over the world they come ... I have waiters who collectively can speak twenty or so languages ... customers have money to spend ... weird in some ways ... family of four sits down ... immediately out come the mobile phones ... check the emails ... text messages ... don't look at anyone at the table ... don't speak to any one at the table ... for all any one knows at the table each of them could be directing a hit on one or more members of the family at the table at any moment ... absolutely nothing human about their facial expressions ... no warmth...no displeasure ... maybe they are all playing online poker with face time app ... so no clues/tells could be sent ... don't look at the menus till shot clock buzzes ... tech has replaced family time ... raising spoiled brats at best monsters at worse ... sorry Mike if I'm unloading ahead of your lunch date ... but I feel you are some one I can be straight with ... a rarity ... and I needed some outlet ... want a drink? ... all this political correctness and now the Black Lives Matter and George Floyd insurrection ... 'Black Lives Matter' sounds like a ten year old came up with that slogan ... really struck with the dull wits of these malcontents ... some refuse to be housebroken ... or maybe they just want to break into houses ... got news for Floyd ... I haven't been able to breathe for years ... can't say this ... can't say that ... but that raid by Homeland Security on the criminal protestors in Portland, Oregon let me breathe a sigh relief, 'I can breathe' ... the calvary finally showed up for the rescue. I thought it only happened in the movies ... Black Lives Matter ... I agree ... but when they resist arrest those lives matter a whole lot less ... I'm in the people business ... so it's easier for me to stay grounded ... would hate to be in front of a computer all day ... real time encounters with customers sharpens my people skills ... computer geeks have such a small world ... stunts their growth."

"You got it Junior ... When I grew up there wasn't social media and all those video games that prepare you for very little ... except it builds an anxiety and addiction to novelty ... and then the perversions of substance abuse ... feel the same way you do about our society ... but of course I notice differences more often because of my older years ... don't worry about your honesty outburst ... I love it ... it's like going back in time ... I stopped watching the main stream media evening news a long time ago precisely because of their lack of animation and honesty that you just so eloquently remarked on ... progressive news anchors speak like robo-callers ... each night it was like going to a wake to witness some 'injustice' ... some nights it was like going out to a row of garbage cans and the news anchor would highlight the garbage under each lid ... always about some injustices ... well if the news is always about injustice how can we be sure that injustice is not actually normal ... if there isn't any news about justice how can we be sure that injustice actually exists? ... anchors always had the voice over with politically correct platitudes and a Kleenex tone ... like a catechism class about their ad hoc religion with exhibits of garbage news as proof ... media has been doing this since the nineteen sixties ... riots in Watts, Detroit, Berkeley ... I was called up for Watts and Berkeley ... I was with the National Guard ... had guns ... but no ammo ... rode around in open flat bed trucks through the night among smoldering buildings and broken glass ... I was young and did what I was told ... no more for me but the rioters got rewarded for their revolution ... they got the Great Society ... we got political correctness and dumbing down children in schools so everyone looks acts and talks like equals ... it's easy for the rioters ... they chant ... 'No justice, no peace' ... I think these near monkeys can only remember four words in a row ... and they want me to take them seriously? ... but they control the agenda because they control the streets or threaten to control the streets ... if the elected government can't enforce law and order then the anarchists will prevail ... I think our politicians have a guilty conscience about their own machinations so they cave in ... and so it goes ... till a vigilante type backlash takes over and settles it ... until then the rioters put numbers up on the score board ... they get what they want ...property owners don't want to live on the streets ... rioters would live on dirt floors...a classic asymmetrical confrontation ... like American troops in Afghanistan wearing uniforms ... and the Taliban wearing regular clothing ... no wonder our troops are always surprised and get killed ... and here another affirmative action program is established along with more money for Nikes ... and gradually the original meritocracy of the country devolves into ghetto law ... the blacks ruined the NBA ... no ref calls traveling any more ... it's ghetto basketball which is more like human bowling knocking away other players who are more like pins, "

Junior interrupted, "... it's not a grievance as much as it is gratuitous vandalism and looting and arson because they don't want to go along with an organized society ... it's a rage against the regularity of the wheel ... they are just grains of sand that screw it all up in the gear box ... they have no talent except to irritate ... it's a stick up ... the media calls it a revolution of freedom fighters or disadvantaged parts of our society ... more misuse of words ... they want to glorify people who create garbage out of other peoples well kept property ... rioters are not worth feeding."

"That's the simple truth, Junior ... in spite of the facts President Johnson responds by pushing through the The Great Society and affirmative action ... he rewards the criminals ... it's like criminal politicians need real criminals as their excuse to govern ... pols are the real criminals ... like they urinate on your pant leg and say it's raining ... and most of the rioters are so stupid ... looking for a chance at free Nikes ... they have the media behind them ... that's a puzzle ... the media thinks they will be exempt on the other side of this revolt if the street morons prevail ... will they be surprised...rioters will steal their cameras and paraphernalia and ship it to Mexico or Taiwan ... it's an inflection point for me ... have guns at home ... looking for self defense gizmos now ... legal stuff ... like pepper spray and batons that open up from five inches to twelve inches with a flick of the wrist ... I ordered three pepper sprays ... ordered a baton but the online vendor notified me I couldn't get the baton delivered in California ... pepper spray is coming ... carjackings happen regularly and assault regularly happens here and officials in Sacramento don't want me to have a self defense weapon ... plus if the thug steals something below a thousand dollars in value there isn't any prosecution ... I have organically developed an appetite for some confrontation ... almost looking forward to an encounter ... frankly would rather go after soft targets like members of government."

Junior jumped in ... "You are getting me in the mood ... I feel like goose stepping ... it wouldn't take much for me to wade in and do serious damage to these bozos ... pity the police ... they take their job seriously and well they should ... media gives them no respect nor do the progressives and liberals ... cops should quietly give the public a taste of what jungle law looks and sounds and feels like and smells like ... you are meeting some one for lunch ... any thing special I can do for you guys?"

"No thanks Junior. Maybe drop by when you are

not busy and meet and chat with us ... you will like my friend ... a Hollywood agent that I have known for many years ... have an idea for a new book ... want some background info from him to flesh out my writing ... have any questions about Hollywood that you were 'afraid' to ask? ... ask my friend Bernie ... he's like talking to me "

"Sounds like an opportunity. Will do." Said Junior.

"I'm having 'Veggies A La Fat Joey' Junior."

"May Fat Joey my dad rest in peace ... I really miss him ... was laid back ... veggies dish is what I like too ... don't eat the crab, shrimp, mussels or the fish ... don't eat sea food that is close to the bottom ... better yet only order food that grows on the land ...water is so polluted ... wholesale fishing side of Alioto's largely sells everything we catch to the Chinese ... they will eat anything ... God those disgusting live or wet markets! ... the fish have better pedigrees than the shoppers ... too many people Mike ... sometimes I pray to Jesus for an asteroid to hit China and bounce into India ... it would be good for the health of the world ... total between those two countries would marginalize close to three billion people ... would be like making the 7/10 in bowling or a hole-in-one ... but Jesus could do it ... he didn't mention birth control while on the planet ... overlooked it ... and I was taught he knew everything ... he had a plan ... yeah right ... but this could be a catch up move ... better late than never considering the plummeting wild places and wild animals ... and the rapidly growing extinctions ... our only hope could be a long shot ... by the way I don't believe in Jesus ... he reminds of Berkeley radicals out of the past."

I almost lost it. It's been ages since I've heard some one rip the human race like an Italian can. "Thanks Junior ... missed that Vesuvius honesty and bombast that only an Italian can put out ... it's in our DNA ... the Chinese have a saying 'The beginning of wisdom is to call things by their right names' ... 'racism' and 'inequality' are words that progressives throw around to cover all problems in our society ... Chinese would say 'overcrowding' is the real problem ... they should know ... originally China looked like Africa before all the Chinese were born and they started eating any thing they could catch ... eventually China looks more now like our domestic stinky Chinatowns only much larger ... their best soil is under the highway ... I predict in the end ...orchards will replace dug up highways ... those Chinese bastards kill my pet cat ... remember some years ago ... the Chinese were exporting cat and dog food that was partially weighted down with melamine so to fudge the protein content? ... by itself it's lethal to small animals ... I read one article that the Chinese were getting their melamine additive from the ashes of burnt coal ... it destroys the liver func- tion when ingested ... I swear I would kill the guilty people in China."

Junior spoke," Overcrowding makes people do things they wouldn't normally do ... it's a matter of physics ... don't get me wrong ... I'm not being philosophical about your beloved pets fate ... I would help you to get even with those scum ... they knew what they were doing to valuable and loved family pets."

Mike continued,"Think about this Junior ... Deoxynbonucleic Acid is in all living things ... it's almost a diabolical formula ... having acid as our base dynamic ... it's like the Myth Of Sisyphus ... the acid organizes our life styles ... only to cut away the progress by design at the same time over a period of tim.e...it's called the aging process ... no wonder we get dementia more and more ... all this change and do's and don'ts ... it wears out our receptors and our brains trying to follow the zigs zags and all that noise from modern day civilization ... the DNA combines and recombines and interacts with other organisms that also combine and recombines with their own acid base ... the net of this is necessarily not pretty ... nothing is for sure ... change is inevitable ... Heraclitus knew that already ... Greek philosophers knew our world intuitively ... modern man only calibrated those facts and monetized them ... we have become simple mechanics ... where are the philosophers?discoveries at the Max Planck Institute in Germany show the Neanderthal was 99.5 % our DNA ... excavated evidence leads to the theory that homo sapiens encountered the Neanderthal about 40,000 ago ... about that same time the Neanderthal started on a road of extinction ... the Neanderthal had existed for 450,000 prior to their demise ... In comparison

Homo Sapiens has only existed for about 60,000 years...the reason that is speculated for the waxing of Homo Sapiens and the waning of Neanderthal was the advanced tool-making ability of Homo Sapiens... these tools were not only helpful for hunting and farming but also for war-making ... Homo Sapiens killed Neanderthals ... first example of genocide ... but there were many more to follow ...

Well here we are in the 21st century with nuclear bombs, biological weapons, high-tech war machine and a generally degraded planet ... don't think we will last as long as the Neanderthal's 450,000 years... what's to be done? ...I suspect that the longevity of our species would be enhanced by looking to the low-tech model of the Neanderthal and adapting their more more basic and conservative approach to survival versus the high-tech arrogant approach ... problem with that is I would bet my life that homo sapiens isn't that wise ...and the only way homo sapiens would accept that outcome would be annihilation and starting all over again ...how about this ironic thought I just had...without memory of the catastrophe...only by looking at fifty thousand year old cave art from now of paintings of twenty-first century man flying a plane ... will our coming distant descendants and our distant relatives try to figure out how we did it ... and then it all starts again with the puzzled cave researchers experimenting ... with kites! "

Junior pops in chuckling, "With acid shaping our evolution? ... it's no wonder we are irritable ...clearly a design flaw … the Greek philosopher Heraclitus said 'No man can enter the same river twice because it's not the same river and he's not the same man'…does that sum it up Mike?"

" You got it Junior…are you Jesuit taught also? … you sell a lot of sea food to China … Junior? … any thoughts on China? … the population just keeps growing…and growing and growing …"

"Yeah Mike I'm Jesuit taught. … mainland China is the biggest threat to to the planet … I'm totally embarrassed to be the same species as the Chinese … they will eat anything … very sad about the Blue Fin Tuna … they can weigh as much as two thousand pounds and swim at forty miles per hour … horses run at fifty-five … and weigh about the same.....the Chinese and the Japanese use sonar and super fast fishing boats to run them down and then kill them … the fishermen are vandals and cowards … the Blue Fin Tuna is better bred and more noble than the humans that kill and consume them…Blue Fin Tuna stock has collapsed … eighty percent of the 'tiger of the sea' have been slaughtered and ended up mostly in some burping Japanese or Chinese stomach … what a way to go…efforts to cut back on the killings have largely come to nothing … what will happen if that fish goes extinct which some are predicting could happen in approximately ten to twenty years? … its a race to take the Blue Fin to the brink while making the most per ounce while the countdown to extinction goes on … it's like Texas Hold'em and table stakes ... an argument for nuclear attack? ... should we and the Russians get together by flanking China and demand they reduce their population over a period of fifty years ... tell them within fifty years they should humanely get to about one hundred million total population ... Premier Xi Jinping could sleep at nights ... and their government would secretly appreciate America and the Russians stepping in to control mainland China population ... actually it would be triangle of power against the Chinese population ... Americans ... Russians ... and the Chinese populations own government ... all in cahoots to humanely cull the herd ... and we and the Russians would chip in with our own humane cull of our population as show of solidarity ... the world sings like a choir about climate change problems ... that's a red herring ... climate change is a symptom ... the real problem is over population ... the governments of the world feel the same way about their constituency as most people feel about a noisy sloppy neighbor ... they wish they would move or get lost ... permanently ..."

"Junior you are a misanthrope like me? ... we are just as bad as the Chinese regarding our disproportionate negative impact on the planet ... over all we have a much smaller population but we consume exponentially more on a per capita basis ... that's why America is so fat ... I think the number we consume is twenty-five percent of worlds gross product but we are only four percent of the worlds population ... but an interesting statistic just recently popped up ... the

Center For Disease Control just published the covid-19 box scores ... and the United States just became twenty-five percent of the infected population on the planet ... the same percent that we consume of the worlds gross output ... it's like nature is keeping track to make sure we pay our fair share of conspicuous consumption by dying at the same twenty-five per-cent rate ... I kind of like it ... it's like some one in power thinks like I do ... I'm in sync with the original layout ... obesity eventually takes care of the problem of obesity. "

Junior continues. "China has a huge appetite for Shark Fin soup and the devastation that brings to shark stocks ... estimates range up to 70 million sharks a year are killed to feed the Asian appetites ... all those newly credit card equipped middle class Chinamen are bewildering to contemplate spoon-ing their soup ... I'm struck by the possible positive side effects of a massive human flu ... but don't think Covid -19 will do the job."

"You mean reducing human population ? Junior."

"Yes Mike ... recently their premier Xi Jinping gave a three hour and twenty-five minute speech to twenty-three hundred delegates of the Communist Party ... it occurs to me right now that the proportional percentage of people in the Chinese government to the population of China is roughly the same as our percentage of congressional representatives to our own population ... same approximate ratio for tyranny no matter the philosophy of government... something to ponder...any way ... Xi Jinping recited his accomplishments and talked about the future with the implication ... who will stop us ? ... he spoke with supreme confidence and theatrical body english-so to speak ... had to be coached...any one who chatters for three hours and twenty-five minutes sounds like a person who is trying to convince the listeners that he's in control ... he also may be trying to convince himself that he's in control ... long story short ... mainland China is too small for its 1.4 billion citizens and China needs to spread out ... they out grew their crib ... China has moved into the South China Sea and has dredged up sea bottom to raise small atolls higher so they can be populated and equipped ...for me it's like putting handicap seats over a toilet seat in the bathroom ... disgusting transformation ...so the atoll becomes like a fishing pier ... and when the fish have all been caught and eaten and eliminated through the humans digestive track there will only be a cesspool left that replaces the South China Sea ... Asian Flus including the latest edition Covid-19 once upon a time kept in check population growth ... also the occasional intramural revolutions or an invasion by the the likes of the Japanese happened ... but not for a long time ... who would want to take on 1.4 bil-lion hungry Chinese? ... the victors, if some how they won would face the same problem Xi Jinping has right now ... how do you feed and house the hoard? ... Africa, Australia and South China Sea are in the sights of Chinese shoppers ... the U.S. should make friends

with Russia...who knows ... we and Russia may need
to flank China for our own and the worlds survival ...
so the clock ticks and the Chinese population expand
... the Chinese population is the existential threat to
the whole planet including themselves ... there has to
be a reduction deal made between China, Russia and
the U.S."

"Let's lighten up the conversation a bit ... tell me
Mike about your Hollywood friend ... can I ask him
simple question like what ever happened to light
entertainment? ... and why are there so many gays
in Hollywood? ... or are the two mutually exclusive
—gays and light entertainment? ... I have seen Frank
Capra and Preston Sturges films on Turner Classic
Movies ... they were throughly refreshing movies ...
actually the intriguing quote,' Dying is easy, comedy
is hard' is attributed to Edmond Gwenn in Capra's
'Miracle On 34th Street' ... true entertainment takes
you somewhere else-pleasantly like a rapture ... I
believe light comedy the best vehicle to deliver my
kind of entertainment by its truthful disarming parts
... it blots out the sour and unhealthy ... it exists for
its own sake ... it is not judgmental or preachy but
merely demonstrates what a happy life might look
like ... one stop succinct honesty wrapped up in quite
satisfying examples ... honesty ... the sine qua non of
sustainable and enjoyable living and entertainment ...
watch a kitten engaging a ball of woolen thread ... the
eyes are riveted ... the claws are digging in or rolling
the ball with gentle swipes ... all the while the kitten

is fixated. ... truth is written on the whiskered face ... if one could write with that witty intensity on any wholesome subject then success is assure ... where has it gone? Indeed comedy is hard, because we are not grateful."

"Interesting comparison Junior. 'Comedy is hard because we are not grateful'. I get your point. Take things as they are ... don't pick it apart ... see the lightness of life ... it's very much a trait of modern man to try to calibrate phenomena and make software to duplicate it so it can be sold on a mass market way...light entertainment doesn't lend itself to formula recreation ... it's in the momen ... it's situational which necessarily needs a buildup and then a climax and then on to the next circumstances ...that's difficult to do ... but if one is not trying to make light comedy a formula for income then it becomes easier because the sequencing fits easier ... it develops ... it's not presented developed which really gets old in a hurry ... have you seen 'My Favorite Year' with Peter O'Toole? It was directed by Richard Benjamin ... I haven't liked Benjamin's other movies ... but 'Favorite Year' was a knee slapper for me ... I was laughing out loud ... sometimes gasping for air ... that doesn't happen to me ... once before ... I had an accident on my horse and broke three ribs in seven places ... I was sore ... tried to be immobile ... turned on TV ... 'The Ernie Kovacs Show' was on ... this is some forty years ago...long story short Kovacs is tied to a wagon wheel and the Indians are shooting arrows ...

missing him ... but for some reason the expression on Kovacs face caught me ... I started to laugh but the more I laughed the more I tried to stop because because my agitating laughter hurt ... it got to the point I started having spasms to the degree my head was turning involuntarily ... I started to look some-what like Kovacs dodging arrows ... and that was the real kicker ... Kovacs and me both in agonizing pain and me laughing and hurting more...it was too too much ... you had to be there Junior to get what I'm saying ... kind of brings into reality comedy as per our definitions of grateful and honesty."

"No. I got it ... what was the O'Toole movie about Mike?"

"It was about an aging actor who could have been modeled after Errol Flynn played by O"Toole ... the old swashbuckler some how guests on a variety show ... the skits are non stop ... they are well done ... the whole cast is Jewish doing Jewish characters... with non stop clipped Jewish humor ... the story goes beyond the TV skits into a Brooklyn enclave of Jews who are the family of one of the key supporting actors in the film itself ... O'Toole goes to dinner there and more more laughs ... check it out Junior."

"I will Mike ... sounds good ... that reminds me ... I saw a review of a book Contempt Of Congress'... it was a dark comedy novella telling the story how an aging hero-like athlete like your O'Toole's example got the news he was dying from a rare blood disease ...

maybe a year to two years to live at most ... so he's motivated and from deep down compelled to make his coming death a challenge for one last competition ... he has always detested politicians ... the hypocrisy and the disingenuous drivel etc ... so he decides to kill as many as he can without getting caught ... one at a time ... different parts of the country ... high value targets are too difficult to get into range ... so he will concentrate on soft targets ... say members of Congress particularly from Blue States like New York and California ... the method will probably be gun sniper ... he did compete in the modern pentathlon ... one of those events was marksmanship ... he scored high in that event ... wants to send a message that one strong willed individual can make a difference ... and the athlete wants to show that being a charlatan in politics carries a risk ... he's looking for dramatic dark happy fun ... he's looking for distraction from his coming death ... and his real purpose is to motivate others to follow his example and join in the cull ... he wants to get the most of the remaining moments he has left ... magnifying those moments into another full life ... change is everything ... time is nothing in comparison ... creatively directing the change is the extra fun ... and the day he dies will be a fine day also."

"Stimulating thought ... if it's written well it could sell." Comments Mike and he continues. "There has been a parabolic increase in threats to politicians ... and I get the feeling that those kind of incidents are being withheld from publication in the hope that they won't be copied and grow faster and maybe lead to actions not just threats ... I recall the Federal Bureau Of Investigation arresting a person who threatened murder to Senator Patty Murray of Washington ... also the F.B.I. announced about a year ago the arrest of a man who threatened to kill both House Speaker Nancy Pelosi and her husband ... trouble in paradise? ... is this the end of the salad days for low talented, no moral compass reps in Congress? ... is there a price for lies, wars without end and binge spending by this criminal class ? ... I hope so ... congress does crimes in a legal way ... by definition to oppose Congress with the same kind of brute force they use is termed illegal ... that's tranny in a raw form right in the open ... but the government has the armed forces to insure their laws are followed ... it's no wonder that the military budget is so high no matter the administration ... the pentagon is the personal body guard of congress ... the forever wars are just to keep in shape before they start killing the citizens to protect the government from getting killed by the citizens ... the people who were involved in the Murray and Pelosi episodes don't appear to be related or commonly organized ... they just had the same idea at the same time ... that's the most dynamic kind of movement ... plans by everyday people happening in a spontaneous way ... lookout if they get organized ... looks like other citizens like me fear the same eventuality of the armed forces."

"Right Mike ... I'm a student of the history of the

Roman Empire I believe what happened to them will happen to us...

Julius Caesar was the first de facto emperor of Rome ... that was in forty-nine B.C.E. ... he was followed by ninety-four more emperors ... the last one was Justin II in 578 C.E ... only thirty-two of the ninety-five died from natural causes ... the rest were assassinated or were killed in battle with opponents who wanted to replace the emperor with themselves ... the reasons for their deaths were the same as why one would kill a tyrant or politician today ... they were not honest and prudent ... they were charlatans ... the main assassins were the Praetorian Guard in cahoots with the Roman Senate ... there are very few individual heroes like Brutus ... the dying athlete in the book is like a Brutus.

... twenty-first century world wide political scene is filled with politicians or regional war lords who would become eager emperors if they had their way ... and where will the assassins come from? ... I'll tell you where they will come from ... the times will make them ... if emperors can get assassinated certainly pencil neck politicians can be eliminated."

"Amen, Junior.

Life is irony ... there 's only one life experience and we all take turns playing different parts as necessary because how circumstances dictate ... congress as criminals ? ... congress routinely moves the parameters of congressional seats to fix the outcomes of election races ... if sporting events were fixed, it would be a crime ... preemptive war by congress is legal ... if someone in the U.S. killed some stranger because he felt threatened, he would be tried for murder ... congress has the power to tax ... if one person asked for money from his neighbor with the threat of confiscation, it would be stealing ... racial discrimination is a violation of the law ... forced desegregation of schools has resulted in math and english proficiency to plummet ... schools are about learning ... not about equality politics. "

"Junior motioned the waiter.I want to buy you a drink Mike. What will it be?"

"Hendrick's Gin martini with a lemon twist, thanks Junior."

"Got it Andy? I'll have a chardonnay. Thanks Andy."

"Junior continued ... The New York Times carried an article about some recently discovered tools of prehistoric man ... they were found in southern Saudi Arabia some one hundred and twenty-seven thousand years earlier than previously thought early humans lived in Africa ... it put into question how long has man been around and where did he come from exactly and where did he go ... most scientist use modern values or assumptions when analyzing early fossil records ... they assume that about 60,000 years ago a group of primates left Africa and colonized the world ... the scientists also figure that early man was energetic ... but if todays species and descendants of early man are at all alike ... I've doubts ... about vigorous energy being applicable when talking about most people ...people stay put and are not about to go for long walks ... particularly if the weather is mild ... or particularly if the weather is poor ...Get me Junior? ... and if it's hot? ... No..way ... of course there were Vikings, Magellan, Columbus and others but they were a tiny minority compared to primal beginnings of man and his history... and they all didn't hail from the equator ... I have a thesis ... suppose about 225 million years ago when all the continents on earth were in one spot — it was called Pangea — man was already present on Pangea in various micro locales ... then the tectonic plates, that were part of the super continent, drifted apart like a moving sidewalk ... our maps of our globe depict the latest continental dispositions and their configurations look like parts of a former assembled puzzle ... if squeezed back together Pangea would reappear ... I think that the moving sidewalks of tectonic plates got people around in a rather lazy fashion witch suits our personalities ... all fruit doesn't drop far from the tree ... what do you think Mike?"

The drinks arrived. "Thanks Andy. Salute Mike."

"Thanks Junior."

The truth has always existed ... but either through misconception, poor language translation or outright lies things have got muddled and confusing

... truth is relatively cheap to maintain ... lies or mis-conceptions require more work and mountains of debt ... truth hangs together ... like your thesis it makes more sense than the conventional thesis ... isn't that the basis of Occams Razor Theory? ... keep it simple ... speaking of change and irony, did you know that Africa now has a middle class of approx-imately three hundred million ... that's roughly the size of our population ... I wonder if they have the percentage of people in government like The United States and China? ... they're buying appliances, TVs, cars, disposable items that are packed in throw away packaging ... where's away? ... supermarkets in the mist ... where did the gorillas go? ... the bourgeois Africans are being added to the recently launched one billion four hundred million Chinese middle class who are munching their way through the planets natural wealth ... an article last week in the New York Times calculated that the total value of financial derivatives in play is approximately five hundred and eighty-four trillion! ... to put that figure in prospective ... com-pare that figure with the approximately twenty trillion dollar value of all real estate in the U.S. ... in other words not only has Wall Street bet all houses on the outcome of their quasi criminal bets on stocks and commodities and bonds and currencies but they have leveraged the real estate at approximately a thirty to one ratio ... Homeric greed with other peoples homes ... commodity prices surge have accounted for the riots around the world ... Wall Street speculators have contributed to poverty and starvation ... you see when poor people buy wheat or gas, they buy it for one day and pay cash ... but when Wall Street "investment" banks and speculators buy wheat or gas, they buy the product of entire fields and refineries for months and years to come ... and they buy it on as little as five percent margin."

"When will the shoe drop Mike? ... how about Africa being a game preserve and the inhabitants being tour guides ? ... the continent is unique ... why try to copy or let the West put it's economic model to work there? ... what does the World Bank know about harmony with nature? ... the World Bank pays off the individual government in Africa and then orders up huge earth moving equipment that rival tectonic plates to destroy the top soil and rivers ...grim news from Kenya this year ... It includes the death of two white Rhinos ... they were slaughtered by poachers for their horns which are used for Asian medicines and Middle Eastern decorative grips on exotic knives ... related news includes the opening of the worlds tallest building — eight hundred meters — in the the North African country of Dubai which is part of the United Arab Emirates ... Dubai is a known user of Rhino horn decoration ... Dubai also defaulted on thirty billion dollars of debt ... Dubai's vast income is not enough ... they have to borrow money to build the worlds tallest structure and also use some per- centage of borrowed moneys to pay for the killing of peaceful endangered animals ... is that the ugliest thing you ever heard? ... it is to me ... my bumper stickers that condemn animal poachers are not working ... barbaric and hubristic events just continue to get worse ... the time for bumper stickers is past ... better to use the whole bumper on some poacher and his guide."

"Junior, I get almost speechless from rage when I hear stories like that ... ever see 'political correctness' reports about the the animal kingdom? ... you wont find it ... but the news media is filled with perceived slights of PC in the human sphere of interest ... but atrocities to hapless animals go on routinely ... scarcely without a word while the bloodless sport of politics gets all the attention ... animals who are millions of years old get less coverage when they are killed but a PC infraction is treated like a forest fire in Yellowstone ... we have a cartoon culture."

"Speaking of cartoons Mike ... I saw Oprah Winfrey in the news recently with more shameless self promotion ... pushing yet another product ... she's wearing a dated wig that I swear white women wore all the way back to the fifties ... she's a lost soul ... she hates being black ... how do I know? ...because she dresses like a white ... straight hair ... it's obvious ... her name always makes me think of some breakfast cereal ... take a gal out of Tupelo, Mississippi ... but can't take Tupelo out of the gal."

"Yeah Junior, I remember her interviewing Sarah Palin when she was exploring a run for the presidency ... Winfrey was the liberal bobble head and

Palin was the conservative bobble head ... shortly afterwards Oprah announced her discontinuing her daytime show ... the ratings didn't support continuing ... Palin was pushing a new book and looking to live in the White House ... one cartoon person going down while another cartoon person was going up ... both caricatures are fit for comic strips ... cartoons are the new normal in politics ... where are the moderates? ... maybe because moderates need nuanced thinking capability from voters whereas cartoon pols can get by and thrive on half brain performance? ... who's going to win ... Biden or Trump?'

"I think Trump Mike ... the reasons why he got elected have only got stronger ... Oprah always is talking about 'redemption' ... anytime a daytime TV host starts talking philosophically she's lost her way ... she's on her way out ... the fat audience doesn't care about philosophy ... I doubt they could define the word ... her guests protest injustice as the reason for their individual predicaments ... most are just sore losers or dim wits ... they do something stupid and now blame the society ... it's more of her philosophy through another person ... dull, dull, dull ...she should have freshened up her show ... Maybe she would still be on the air ... she could have interviewed Khalid Sheikh Mohammed ... wow would she get a high rating with that guest ... he was the architect of 9/11...Khalid pleaded guilty ... He said, 'We don't want to waste our time with [legal] motions. All of you are paid by the U.S. government and I'm not trusting any American' ... It was a rare example of someone taking responsibility for his actions ... and the responsibility will amount to an execution ... his statement was unlike the routine guests that Winfrey paraded through ... Khalid is unlike our overpaid weenie executives throughout American industry ... or all the other countless "victims" in our weenie society ... and that includes all those black monsters who are on Death Row for brutal murders but blame a "racially prejudiced legal system" for their troubles ... why doesn't Oprah Winfrey do a remote broadcast from Gtmo with Khalid? ... she could expose her fat, dumb and bored viewing audience to a real person ... redemption is her religious mantra ... what could be more honest than Khalid wanting a honest resolution to an ugly affair? ... she didn't do it because she is a dull dumb person ... but she is a tireless worker ... that's what made her so successful ... plus she was African American which gave her cachet with dumb corporations who sponsor her show with ad dollars ..."

Mike asked," ... where are the moderate politicians Junior? ... Trump and Biden are both swinging for the fences for their base ... If only some one would advocate moderation ... the biggest force on the planet is gravity ... gravity is a moderating influence ... Bruce Lee knew that ... and before him Isaac Newton knew that ... instead of fighting gravity work with it's perpetual influence ... gravity is that unseen hand that controls everything on the planet ... no matter the time zone ... no matter the race or religion

...we are all tethered and molded by gravity ... mountains rise just so far ... rivers and streams meander uniformly ... objects drop at the same speeds ... pay respect to gravity and gravity will be a useful ally ... smaller buildings smaller cars smaller families ... more open space ... less government weight at the top ... gravity has logic and doesn't lie ... go to sleep at night and wake to the same gravity ... if you can understand that ... one can plan better ... along with gravity is the ubiquitous Golden Ratio ... in numbers it is 1.618 ... it's the ratio of length to width ... the Greeks called it Phi ... the ratio is the most pleasing to the eye ... this ratio is found in nature and in the universe ... it is observed so often that it is a clue to how the cosmos is laid out and operates ... plant cell structures have it ... our bodies have it ... buildings have it ... spiral galaxies have it ... I think it is related to gravity which is related to motion ... if you exist you must have a sustainable basic form ... ergo the Golden Ratio is the starting point ... go with it ... the fibonacci sequence contains Phi ... which is the ratio of each paired sequence of numbers ... for example 5 divided by 3 equals 1.618 or PHI ... there must be a Phi ratio between successful actors ... maybe in the cadence of speaking to each other or the height ... or the camera angles which is not natural but can fool the audience ... food for thought and an experiment to be tried."

Junior responded, "... unseen hand ... right ... it's not god ... it's gravity that limits height ... it limits weight ... Einstein thought about gravity a lot ...he then used his thoughts to back into his time and relativity theory ... but I don't think there is time as such ... there is only change ... no change ... no time ... and change implies motion ... and for me the force of gravity is a function of how fast the mass is traveling ... a parked cement truck does not have the force of gravity a cement truck going fifty mile per hour ... park a bicycle beside a cement truck ... then let that same truck at fifty miles per hour motor by you ... you will notice the difference ..."

Mike has an idea, "... only motion creates a book on a shelf has no power ... but read the book ... then things happen ..." Mike continues ... "like our news media ... it has news to present ... it can present the news in a number of ways ... straight facts? ... but that could be boring and send listeners to other channels ... or they can present the news in an inflammatory way ... that would assure to make some viewers hang around a bit longer to see what's next to be said...and that's how ratings are achieved ... that's how money is made for the media ... that's how anchor news people make millions in yearly salaries ... present news that is out of touch with facts ... in a word 'lie'...or another word that is increasingly used to distort news is 'omit' and 'distort' ... lying speaks for itself ... but omitting facts ... taking facts out of context which then distorts ... quoting only parts of the quote can change entirely the message of the news piece ... then it can become inflammatory ... why do the national TV

anchors get paid millions?...because they are the cat-
alyst or the moving force to purposely move the news
in a compelling way due to the charm of the anchor...
but beware of TV anchors who are paid exorbitant
amounts of money ... paying anchors like high paid
Hollywood actors is a red flag of attempted theft of
the truth...news reporting should be straightforward
... but when someone like long gone Katie Couric is
paid fifteen million per year there is something else in
play ... ratings and market share of CBS is that something else ... if the ratings aren't high enough then
sponsors will not spend millions to advertise on CBS
... If that happens then CBS will not make millions in
profits and Couric will not make her millions either ...
this market share and ratings game also has a direct
influence on how and what news will be presented
... for example in the pursuit of viewers the nightly
news will be presented in an unchallenging dumbed
down type of format ... the 9/11 terror attack was presented as a validation of American foreign policy in
the Middle East ... question? ... wouldn't a better
U.S. foreign policy have precluded such a disaster?
... has the news over the years about the Middle East
been doctored to retain popular American concepts
?... but the requirement of keeping market share pre-
vents challenging the viewers with questions about
national direction and the goals of foreign policies
in all its intricacies and maybe changing policies ...
who is setting policy? ... companies have products for
sale ... report news that may add sales of detergents
to a mass market isn't a way to inform about issues

of life and death ... in essence the news is presented in such a way to mesh with popular ideas so products are sold ... in other words the news has been presented after poll results tally what viewer expect in the news...that's not news reporting ... that's poll reporting ... the roots of a liberal media are imbedded in the quest to increase market share of the news vendor ... wrong priority ... telling people about the facts of a story is comparatively dull ... but adding reasons ... real or imagined ... behind the facts of the story ... add discrimination as a reason behind the story and immediately the story has legs ... it will tap into a baited audience ... any subject has a yin and yang ... the editor of the news vendor has to pick one side ... market share necessarily demands that the news organization seek out the lowest common denominator ... of readership ... that also helps ad sales with mass marketers ... so routinely we end up with stories that glorify or support generally the have nots against the haves ... even if there are no "haves" the editor would have to invent one to have a target for his "have nots" ... and then comes the politicians who declare 'If I'm elected I will address this unbalanced situation to the reward of the discriminated' ... George Bernard Shaw said, 'Most people shouldn't have been born ... news editors would never allow that Shavian truth to guide their publishing efforts ... ergo that's why we are where we are."

Junior responds, "... how much must we grieve over racial or sexual issues ... that question was asked and answered some time ago by the producers at the PBS NewsHour ... they answered 'how much time do we have?' ... So in place of news came black and gay anecdotal stories from around our country on a regular segment dedicated to those subjects ... it was like an Uncle Toms Cabin sequel ... by the way Uncle Toms Cabin was a best seller in the middle of the nineteenth century ... second only to the bible ... Abraham Lincoln is quoted as saying Harriet Beecher Stowe started the Civil War ... Stowe was a christian missionary ... no President Lincoln ... you started the Civil War by squeezing the south with unfair taxes and tariffs ... slavery was a side issue ... no one goes to war to free the kitchen help or free the cotton pickers ... I think he was our worst president followed by Lyndon Johnson ... both presidencies dealt inappropriately wth race issues at the expense of a unified country ... so white matron Judy Woodruff who is the senior editor of the NewsHour along with a handful of her harpy identity politics icons offer their banal tripe of 'injustice to victims' with quasi Kleenex voices in a soap opera style ... I remember the night I stopped watching the NewsHour ... that nights feature story was a black lisping homosexual man on a Texas University campus ... he was a 'two-fer' both colored and gay ... gushing ... he was some what depressed ... he bemoaned his place in life ... black and homosexual and most of the campus was not ... that's it ... that was his burden and sorrow like an abandoned pet bird in a cage looking at an empty seed bowl and an empty water feeder ... end of segment ... no more ...

so what was I supposed to do? ... reach out? ... send him a valentine? ... organize a GOFUND charity for gender reassignment surgery ... is this news? ... do the contributors to the NewsHour have this trite piece in mind when they give?... is there a bubble in liberal news media coverage about black and gay issues? ... poor senior news editor matron Woodruff ... with a face to match her empathetic voice ... she sums up in her drawn face the grim segment ... somewhat like Grant Woods 'American Gothic' painting but without the charm."

Mike comments, "... progressives remind me of a gang of Don Quixote's ... seeking and tilting at normality ... doing gods work with their civil rights act religious hand book ... I can't talk to them anymore ... I just ignore their conversations in the flesh or in social media ... if it weren't for mainstream media the whole ugly civil rights era wouldn't have started or have lasted ... It's part of Hollywood culture being fed daily through the news vendors ... they never stop ... that's the essence of propaganda ... repeat repeat repeat ... Hollywood will not change ... they are dedicated to making everyone else change."

Junior interrupted, "... it's not Hollywood alone ... they are helped by Marxist-Leninists and the Christian religion which is a form of communism ... in the day of Jesus when there were only two hundred and fifty million to five hundred million world population the effects on the planet were really not a topic ... but now with almost eight billion on the planet ... there has to be a better reason to help any of them than just because they want charity ... humanity at this volume of population is more like a lethal plague ... frankly ... the idea that government will provide more individual rights and more charities going forward despite almost eight billion humans isn't realistic ... population and individual rights are going to contract by necessity ... and the government will not be relevant if it doesn't actively pick a side ... if it doesn't take sides then it will suffer the fate of the losing side of the population. "

Mike raises his glass" ... good drinks Junior ... you are right on the christians and their religion that smacks of socialism ... more than smacks ... it's pure strength socialism ... I wrote an article on that about fifteen years ago ... as I recall the Bible mentions poverty 3000 times ... Christ personally talked about helping the poor on many occasions ... if one were to sum-up the Bible's main message it would necessarily be to 'help the poor' ... Christ was relevant to the people of his time because of that connecting message ... poverty is a quality of life issue ... which brings in the question of poverty in the modern age and the issues of life prolonging medicines and the resulting issues of quality of life and termination of life ... modern medicine has a two sided impact on the quality of life ... from fertility drugs that enhance conception through antibiotics that fight life-threatening diseases to questionable life prolonging techniques that can prolong life for an indefinite period...the other aspect of modern medicine is the overcrowding and the resulting pressure on natural resources that it effects ... zero sum planet ... one species gain is another's potential loss ... creationists or evolutionists would have no argument on that fact ...t his is the question Junior ... does modern man do god's work when he helps people have an improved quality of life? ... whether you believe in god or the golden rule one would answer yes ... but on the flip side does modern man do god's work when he encourages child bearing ... provides life saving drugs and prolongs life artificially without consideration to the quality of life? ... fifty percent of childhood deaths in Africa are caused by malnutrition ...

... if modern man and his medicine want to fight poverty and provide quality of life at the same time then it becomes an imperative for medicines two-sided impact to be addressed ... if man wants to play god ... keep in mind that god allowed for deaths in a natural way ... "

Junior turns it over in his mind according to his facial clues and responds "... like most questions on religion ... you either believe in god or you don't ... if one doesn't believe in god..than my advice would be to avoid asking questions like that to any believer... for that matter it's best to avoid believers at parties if one is trying to have fun at the party ... "

Mike chuckled. "I learned that lesson a long time ago ... interestingly the Christian religion was accepted by the Roman Emperor Constantine in 313 C.E. through the Edict Of Milan ... ten years later it became the official religion of the empire ... it sounds to me like a shotgun marriage ... the ancient Roman Empire collapsed in 476 C.E. ...simply they ran out of money and influence and like all occupiers they eventually have to go home ... it's cheaper and more peaceful at home ... the adoption of Christianity was a move of desperation to collect taxes ... but that didn't fix the problem ... it's much the same what's happening with us today in America ... we need more money and to that end we make citizenship easy to attain and the welfare state grows so the government stays in power ... and fiat money and debt fills the gap until everyone bails out because the checks don't cash because the money is worthless ... it's like having one foot on the dock and the other on a boat that's drifting away from the dock ... the original Roman republic and the following empire lasted about one thousand years ... Constantine let the Christians have official status in 313 C.E. and he was able to add another one hundred and sixty years to the total ... it didn't look pretty at the end with King Alaric and his Visigoths sacking the enclave Rome in 410 C.E ... that what was left of the empire ... but the church went on to greater glories with it's influence on kings and emperors of Europe until pedophiles took over or covered up the crimes ... Nero was smart ... he absorbed the Christians church to hedge his position as emperor ...he wanted one foot in the present and one in the afterlife ... so to control expectations ... "

Junior commented ..." I read an Al Jazeera article by some Middle East sage ... remarked that Americans only learn about religions, geography and history by going to war ...

... Did you know that Muslims believe Mahdi will return soon to cleanse the world of infidels? ... he will then establish a universal Islamic rule ... he sounds like the Judeo-Christian Messiah ... Scholars believe that both the Mahdi and the Messiah are loosely based on Ahura Mazda ... that was the supreme god of the 6th century B.C. Persian prophet Zoroaster ... attempts to form a new government in Iraq are also proving to be educational ... it would appear that mutually exclusive political tribes are trying to form a government in a future Iraq that will allow those tribes to remain mutually exclusive ...

maybe the lesson to be drawn is that mutually exclusive tribes will not fit into a democratic paradigm ... in future the worlds people will probably end up belong to various tribes ... because the cost of central government is more expensive than local government ... which is more efficient and adaptive... and barter will be the medium of exchange ...doesn't leave much if any room for central government ... it probably obviates a national media ... local news will be more important" ...

"I throughly believe that Junior ... it's hard enough managing a family rather trying to manage an empire ... that's were fiat money comes ... our politicians have a guilty conscience ... that's why they came up with fiat money ... only they know for sure how rotten they are ... and the more rotten they are the easier it is to intimidate them ... the rioters certainly know that much about politics ... they are smarter than generally assumed ... their problem is coming up with valuable contributions to society ... too busy gaming the system."

"Tell you what Mike ... I don't have a guilty conscience...if it comes to politicians or rioters ... as far as I'm concerned I'll take them out equally ... I don't like either."

Mike just looked at Junior's intensity and was impressed. He had that impression when they first met that a generational and culture change was in the making. He just got confirmation ..." What's the plan Junior?"

"You are looking at the floor plan Mike ... right here ... Alioto's would be home base ... I have no idea how far the society will unravel ... if it unravels ...but this is a building for housing ... and it's a business for feedin ... out there are boats for supplies ... fishing ... or counter attacks ... I have thirty employees whom I trust and who also are capable of most anything ... all totaled it's a place to start all over no matter the paradigm ... from the looks of the possible opponents we are in good shape logistically and weapons ..."

Mike asks. "Who would be your opponents?"

"Not the police ... so already I have calvary to help me and my team and property ... I offer food and support as I'm capable of providing ... the rioters really only have the main stream media and attorneys ... neither of which would show up for real confrontation ... maybe I could do a clandestine raid on the local news vendors ... how would they feel if their camera and support equipment were smashed beyond repair ... would they buy new equipment? ... would the news people still want a job if they got new equipment but would still face possible physical injury? ... and if they did come back ... then the next level would be sniper activity against the media ... and then it would be case closed ... the unknown is whether we here on the wharf could bring others around the country on board with the revolt? ... I'm suspecting the prospect of others handing the keys to their homes and business' over to rioters and their attorneys would be dismissed out of hand ... they would be pushed to follow my lead."

"Valid points ... all valid points Junior ... I like especially attacking the media ... they are the real instigators of unrest ... Covid-19 could end the progressives philosophy ... it could end up being a lesson in politics and philosophy that no one will ever forget ... and the lesson is only one winner ... fiat money allows multiple winners ... but there can only be one winner ... that includes the conservatives learning that lesson also ... since Franklin Roosevelt and the New Deal democrats and some republicans answered each challenge with another government tax and spend program ... it's been going on for over eighty years ... the debt has so many zeros that 's it's embarrassing ... when we get a true crisis like Covid-19 money has no effect as a solution ... yet they crank out more money ... politicians and particularly the progressives refuse to choose opening up the society and the predictable increase in some deaths ... those platitudes of 'saving one life is more important' is plain nonsense ... fact is the economy must survive for all to benefit ... get me Junior?"

"Yeah I think so Mike. Because if that happens it is an implied acknowledgement that working people are more important than people with disabilities ... which in turn blows up their whole welfare philosophy ... which includes civil rights and equality schemes etc...."

"Junior, you got it ... in the end money is only a tool ... it's not the end all ... teach kids important skills ... forego social engineering."

"Mike ... what's your Hollywood friend think of black actors? ... and does he represent any?"

"I don't know Junior. ... does he have any clients who are black? ... I don't know ... problem I have with blacks on stage or on screen is I can't make out their emotions on their faces ... looking at black is not the same as looking at white ... black doesn't reflect ...white illuminates features. ... it's like whites have their own lighting on board ... black lighting is a whole different challenge ... directors and the lighting crew have to make special lighting angles with more powerful accurate lights to high light black faces ... John Ford said believable dramatic acting starts with what the eyes are doing and saying ... getting to what a negroes eyes are saying requires illuminated close ups ... with that in mind negro faces require close-ups with powerful lights ... I have heard how some of the lovely sex goddess' of Hollywood complained of burned skins by baby spots and Klieg lamps ... I think blacks would experience same discomfort ... more close ups with black actors makes this happen ... close ups of Hollywood beauties is fine but close ups of black action hero is quite another view ... so I would think roles would be fewer ...

...Porgy And Bess comes to mind ... lovely music by George and Ira Gershwin ... but that's where it stops ... I can't make out the dark faces on the screen or stage ... the story is about victims which is not entertainment for me ... blacks and stereotyped 'victim' roles really really gets old ... the opera was written in 1925 ... roughly sixty years after the Civil War and roughly forty years beforeThe Civil Rights Act Of 1964 ... and now roughly fifty-five years after the legislation we are all still talking about black victims ... all tallied it's been one hundred and fifty-five years and we are still talking about reparations for slavery and black is still a hot topic ... and during all that time slavery still exists in Africa ... white folk have become enslaved to political correctness ... and blacks and all their supporters are the masters of burning, looting and tearing down statues that don't belong to them ... I wonder what the Gershwin's would think of the blacks today ? ... in sum ... Junior for me ... everything is as it should be...in short ... want less friction? ...write less laws that profess to promote harmony... lawyers will distort the best intentions of written laws ... because laws are on paper and are immovable ... whereas attorneys are free to attack at the perimeters and eventually cause more strife than the law promised to avoid ... "

"Mike I have to get back to work..most enjoyable talk ... I will try to drop by and meet your friend if that's alright."

"Please do Junior.. it's been fun and stimulating ... my friend is due." Mike looked out across the bay.

Mike looks out to the Bay scene before him.

Chapter XII
San Francisco's 1960's Entertainment

Between Tiburon and the Golden Gate Bridge is the little town of Sausalito. I think the town name translates into "little willow trees". It's beautifully situated in the lee of the prevailing westerly wind which can be cold and windy.

At Sausalito's sea level there are many restaurants and shops. Then it rises maybe five hundred feet. The slopes are built up with lovely homes that have breath taking views covering about one hundred and eighty degrees. In the nineteenth-seventies there were numerous dinner and dancing clubs by the shore. Ondine's and Scoma's were side by side at water level. Some clubs had first class entertainment. I remember seeing The Vince Guaraldi Trio at the Trident. They had two big hits among many other well done selections. The hits were "Cast Your Fate To The Wind" and "A Taste Of Honey".

San Francisco had more venues and consequently

bigger audiences. Particularly The Hungry 'I" was my favorite. Owner/impresario Enrico Banducci said the "I" was short for "Id" which he said appealed to intellectuals. I saw the Kingston Trio and comedians Shelly Berman and Bob Newhart and singer Kay Starr there. Club owner Banducci had an eye and ear for talent. There were few venues any where that matched the great talents that got their start at the Hungry "I".

The Hungry "I" had among others Mort Sahl, Woody Allen, Ronnie Schell, Bill Cosby, Barbara Streisand, Lenny Bruce, Tom Lehrer, The Limelighters, Ike And Tina Turner, John Phillips led the "i"'s house band "The Journeymen". Phillips went on to create the Mama's and the Papa's.

Of all the acts that have performed at the Hungry "i" my favorite comedian was Mort Sahl. His act was somewhat like humorist Will Rogers of the nineteen twenties and thirties. Rogers would always say "All I know is what I read in the newspapers". Sahl would come on stage with a newspaper and then just read it as printed with his seemingly spontaneous witty and satirical and caustic comments. His voice and cadence were very dry. You could hear a pin drop. It all was absorbed by the audience. He teased the article so to speak to get what was in it that sounded disingenuous. He didn't point out the laugh line. The audience wanted to take that honor themselves.

During the early sixties his star was shining brighter and brighter. Then he added President John

F Kennedy and the Viet Nam War to his caustic dry wit monologue.

JFK's father Joe Kennedy Sr. was livid. Kennedy had millions and had many political and theatrical connections. The senior Kennedy was a former boot-legger and then a stock market manipulator and then a banker in that order. If one is a bootlegger, a part of that business includes killing or fighting the com-petition for control of territory. "Buy my booze or else" was the sales pitch bootleggers laid down. So with that in his resume he had no moral authority or qualms of conscience for going after Mort Sahl for merely telling the truth about his son and his admin-istration. Kennedy got Sahl blackballed to the point he couldn't get work. Ironically Sahl is still working on a limited basis at a small theater in Mill Valley, California to this day. Kennedys are gone and Sahl is still working—doing his humor like only he can. Still doing the classic Sahl monologue. He was right about JFK being incompetent and he was right about the utter stupidity of Viet Nam War which included biolog-ical warfare Agent Orange and using napalm on the people in that agrarian country.

My favorite singing group at the"i" were the Kingston Trio. I think they did two albums live at the "i". They had voices and confidence and great per-sonal arranging because they were intelligent and didn't do drugs or booze to excess. Three men with three instruments exponentially entertaining.

Pianist/singer Buddy Greco was at the Purple Onion. I think stripper Tempest Storm also entertained there when Greco wasn't. The Purple Onion had quite a list of later big stars getting a first start at that club. The list includes Alameda, California housewife Phyllis Diller stretching to Richard Proyor stretching yet again to Maya Angelou to double stretch to Jim "Gomer Pyle" Nabors to The Irish Rovers and The Smothers Brothers (Then a Trio) who did their first album there called "The Smothers Brothers At The Purple Onion." Owners/managers Keith Rockwell and Virginia and Irving Steinhoff were quite the eclectic impresarios. People like they and Enrico Banducci of The Hungry "I" were the creative genius's made it all happen. Both clubs only seated about one hundred. Quite remarkable. Top entertainment served up in a personal way. A far cry from todays stadium size venues filled with crazies.

Bill Graham Presents had a long list of a harder rock groups parade through his venues of Winterland and Fillmore West Auditorium in San Francisco. They included The Grateful Dead, Jefferson Airplane, Big Brother And The Holding Company with Janis Joplin and Otis Reading. There were many more. I didn't go to those venues. The hippies smelled and their clothes were dirty. I think there is an inverse relationship between civil rights and personal cleanliness. The more civil rights granted the less of personal hygiene is observed. Any one who is odoriferous will lose my patience. I don't tolerate conversation that is preceded with a visage of slovenly dirty clothing.

It seems now after looking back on the hippies and their philosophies how juvenile they mostly were. The air of sophistication that they tried to project was a mock hip fabrication that they crouched behind. Any accepted custom in the culture at that time was immediately met with skepticism with a brief comment of "why" or "why not?" and that was it. No matter the custom the judgment was always "why have this custom". The retort was a judgment that the custom had no value. Yet there was no explanation of what was wrong with the custom. Just a mocking attitude. It was acting. It wasn't wisdom. Ask a hippy why his clothes were dirty. The answer would be "why not?".

It lasts today. Look around. Sniff the air. Less talk about filth. More talk about civil rights shortfall. And then they start burning and looting. Evidently other peoples personal property is for sharing or destroying if the looters hasn't got enough. The looters never have enough because they mostly don't work. Unless it's working at stealing. And the looters want fairness in wealth. Many of the progressives and liberals come from fathers and mothers who were hippies. Fruit doesn't fall far from the tree.

Later in life Bill Graham became friendly with Director Francis Ford Coppola. Coppola of the "Godfather" movies. Coppola had Graham do cameos in two films——"Apocalypse Now" and "The Cotton Club". I remember in 1989 when the devastating Loma

Preita earthquake hit the Bay Area. Graham organized a benefit presentation of many rock stars including a super personality from many eras —- Bob Hope. All proceeds went to the needy which there were many.

Jo Stafford past away some years ago. She was ninety. She was eulogized by musical critics ".... as the woman with a pure vibrato-less voice, with perfect intonation that conveyed steadfast devotion and reassurance with delicate understatement". I have an album with her and the Pied Pipers backing up Frank Sinatra with the Tommy Dorsey Band. I have also heard and enjoyed her album. The musical critics are correct. But one has to listen to her to really be informed and moved. The eulogy can't cover her talent adequately.

Last night an older David Bowie concert was shown on TV. I looked and listened for as long as possible. It took about a minute for an earful. His "singing" could have been played backwards with the same effect.

There exists another inverse relationship between quality music and the growth of population. I.E. the more the people the worse the quality of music becomes. So when the over-due-die-back of the human infestation finally happens there will be rewards. I think Jo Stafford's excellence will out last David Bowie's whatever he calls what he did.

Chapter XIII
Bay Area Prehistoric To Present

It's the beautiful expansive windswept San Francisco Bay that makes the city so attractive. Port cities are the hubs. Whether here, Seattle, Los Angeles, Portland, New Orleans and New York. People come and go and the port cities are never the same. Like malleable clay that never dries new cultures spring up. Food, music, clothing constantly evolving. Some changes come and go quickly. Some stay and become permanent. The changes that linger have the common thread of symmetry. Beauty and utility have to be symmetrical to last. They are recognizable. The functioning pattern is apparent. Which inspires a variation on that design—-shorter lines of connectivity. Brief is better in talking and clothes design. And this offers more inspiration and creativity and so on. The wind and the water and earthquakes constantly sculpt the land to a underlying metaphysic. Hexagons, circles, triangles, rectangle and squares etc. And then back again sometimes in a day, week, month.year or multiplied by parts of all durations forever.

Twenty thousand years ago the entire planet was engulfed in an ice age. The water had frozen and the sea level was much lower. So much lower that our coastline now was thirty mile due west. Todays Farallon Islands were actually hills on the ancient coastline. The area that was to become the San Francisco Bay was then a large river valley. The river was taking the draining water of the Sierra Nevada mountain range along a thirty mile route to the old coastline. The lush valley supported a riot of wildlife. It include the small to the large. The large animals included Saber Tooth Tigers, American Lions, bears, camels, buffaloes, llamas and ground sloth.

About eleven thousand years ago the ice started to melt. Six thousand years later the sea level had risen by three hundred feet. The San Francisco Bay had arrived. And here I am in Alioto's Restaurant on San Francisco's Fisherman's Wharf. Waiting for a friend to talk about society and movies and politics and have fun.

In those same twenty thousand years ago till today the calculus remains the same— —hunt or flee. But now we hide behind noisy deceptive legal talk. We defeat adversaries by the process. No quick kills. Just exhaust your enemies by false accusations. Delay justice. Attorneys love billable hours. We don't have "loser pays" form of law. There's no cost, relatively speaking, to sue some one. Cowardly attorneys hide behind words and have no threat to them financially because theres no "losers pays" in our courts. That's the definition of a "cheap shot". But the cheap shot could turn into a bankruptcy for parties to a law suit. But no bankruptcy for the attorneys. They have no liability. Just quote some book on a shelf that says it's the law and they have a thriving business. Cowards all. There were no lawyers twenty thousand years ago. There were no lawyers one thousand years ago. Our modern day lawyers are a modern phenomena. They rose to power at the same time congress rose to power. I'm surprised more attorneys aren't killed on a regular basis by financially ruined defendants or screwed clients who were victims of bad judgment by their legal representative. A physical attack of revenge is more affordable and gives more satisfaction than hiring a fifteen-hundred dollar a hour attorney.

How many movies have been made in San Francisco? Why S.F. ? It has a natural setting that projects drama and it's free for the directors and camera man. Film noir were shot here in black and white. Color is distracting. Black and white is dramatic and philosophical. Plus there is a wide assortment of cultures and cuisines that beckons producers of motion pictures to drive or fly from Los Angeles to San Francisco. I hate to use the word diversity because it's been overused and misused as a goal. But diversity as a draw works well on midways at a circus. And modern day San Francisco has a diverse midway some might say dizzying midway of assorted odd or illegal people. A thousand years ago there were no restaurants or martinis or table cloth. The living only had the moment without structure but they had wit and an instinct for survival.. They tried to survive and not be seen or heard by predators. Talk takes energy. One might need that extra energy to flee or chase.We are a long way from the real world of those days.

Since the 1960's Civil Rights legislation, its fair to say that public school teaching goals have been switched from the pursuit of excellence to the pursuit of inclusion. To be clear, the progressives philosophy constructively teaches that advancement in learning is only worthwhile if all advance. That's why we got Affirmative Action. Basically the progressives say the individual is less valuable than the collective which in reality is the state saying the state is more important than the individual or the collective. Can you follow this? The state uses the majority to intimidate the the minority. But the majority follows the instructions of the state. Try explaining what I just said to any one you choose. Most will have their eyes roll or change the subject.

The Civil Rights Act has become a tool for extortion in its more extreme examples. Like burning and looting in the recent example of George Floyd riots for "justice". We were a meritocracy. Now in the pursuit of inclusion and equality we drifted into identity politics.Which ironically is a form of racism which the Civil Rights Act sought to stop. Individual excellence has constructively become elitism and not to

be celebrated. Our top students most now idle until the most obtuse student in the class catch up. This is particularly difficult with some students from foreign countries who are here legally or illegally "don't get it". Slower witted students should be segregated into a less demanding curriculum.

But this "don't get it" problem also applies to minorities that the Civil Rights Act Of 1964 was directed at. Particularly the boys are a problem. But they do understand one thing about the new goals of the U.S. teaching. They know that the minorities really control the agenda. So if they don't get the lessons or don't excel in the lessons or they just don't want to get it, they can effectively hold everyone back as an exercise of power. Perhaps the burden of equality in schooling is too much for them and they resort to a kind of nihilism towards education in general as a cover up. Maybe they just don't like the regularity of the wheel. Or in their terms they don't want to be called for traveling by a referee in a National Basketball Association game. They prefer ghetto ball.

Care giving is not an occupation for smarter children. They should be segregated from the nihilists. Consequently everything is as it should be. There's isn't systemic racism as much as there is blow back from laws which tell people who they must associate with. Or what opinion one should have about people.

LGBTQ+ is under the umbrella of the Civil Rights Act. So some men become women and trample the competition and the sports laws at the same time.It's an egregious unintended consequence of laws that should not have been written. It's proof we are going in the wrong direction in this equality quest. Not only fencing but track and field also.Women haven't a chance in that kind of new and equal competition.

Here's a bizarre application of the philosophy of the Civil Rights Laws in sports competition. When does a cripple's crutch make him more competitive than an able bodied athlete? Answer : when a double-amputee uses the trademarked Cheetah Flex Foot.

South African Oscar Pistorius was granted the right to try out for the Olympic games. The liberal Court Of Arbitration For Sport created in 1984 recently overturned the 1912 founded International Association Of Athletic Federations' definition of an illegal apparatus. The illegal apparatus was the Flex Foot. It was indeed a performance enhancer that was unfair to normal competitors.

Sounds familiar. And now unfair affirmative action has made a beachhead in the Olympic Games in the form of hybrid technology. Cheetah gives Oscar, who is already 30 pounds lighter because of the missing limbs below the knee, the ability to run down the track on ultra- light carbon fiber blades that effectively mimic pogo-like springs attached to his thighs. There is less wind resistance with the blades, there are never the problems of sore feet or sore lower leg muscles. Also with less body mass, the vital dynamic of oxygen distribution is concentrated in a smaller muscular areas.

Enough already. With the human population approaching 8 billion on the planet we should be celebrating excellence and not degrading the heretofore ultimate physical competitions of the Olympic games. Handicapped people have their own Paralympian games. Oscar should stay where he belongs.

Rioters about past slavery are in the streets along with rioters who rage against the wheel along with rioters who rage against laws and the police.

Technology that obviated human slavery has continued to advance it's capabilities to the point masters of human slaves have now become slaves of their own technology creations. How's that for irony? I propose changing the word "nature" to the word "irony". The eternal recycling of the universe necessarily produces new from old. My observation is use a tool and lose your place.Natural law is filled with irony.

"And the proud will be humbled".That's from the Bible. But better than that verse is the Greeks aphorism" Nothing To Excess". Irony, as usual pops up.The inventors of tools have in fact replaced themselves. Use a tool and replace yourself. Natures metaphysic always keeps score. It declares "Want to work less?" OK. Then invent work avoiding gadgets.But at some point, you inventors will make yourselves redundant and you will beg for novelty because of your boredom.

Hello Las Vegas. Hello Hollywood. Hello pornography. Hello obesity. Hello alcoholism. Every eighteen billion year old time tested metaphysic that the human eliminates through technology will at some time in the future be reinvented by the human in the search for survival and peace of mind—-if they are still around.

Before there was work saving technology there was slavery. Slavery is the philosophical template for the eighteen century industrial revolution. Look at what happened. Imported slaves that were sold by their own families and tribal leaders have now ironically shed their sixteenth, seventeenth, eighteenth and nineteenth century physical chains and exchanged them for work saving affiliations with progressive politics. Those aggregates led by carpetbaggers have quasi enslaved the former slave owners through welfare state taxes. Now the former slaves have become fat, alcoholics, Hollywood film junkies, leading pornographic lives. They become what they deplored. They now have boredom because they are not useful to anyone else except as a vote caster for progressive politics. They are not useful to themselves. They have lost their place. So it would appear that slaves and slave owners have misused the original advantages of slavery and technologies to the point both classes of people are largely redundant. The animals they slaughter to feed themselves have a better pedigree and are more noble then the humans that feast on them. Avoiding work points out that all things considered a hands on personal honest days work is the best way to live.

Chapter XIV
What's Different About Todays Riots

There is something new about this latest install-
ment of unhappy African-Americans rioting. It
is mean. It is organized. To me there are professional criminal planners behind the seemingly
spontaneous rioters. The targeted cities are usually
run by progressive city administrations who think the
rioters should have some time to blow off steam. The
police are instructed to have a hands off approach.
And of course the mainstream media is the choir.
There are laws still on the books that looting and
arson are criminal offense that police could use deadly
force. Not now. The Civil Rights Act has become an
extortion tool against capitalism. The rioters seem to
be following a communist tactical street philosophy.
But that tactic is inside the Trojan Horse of civil rights.
The eternal fact remains, they who control the streets
control the country.

What really is amazing is that wealthy progressives have bought into the communist plan. They

have no idea what communism can do to their bourgeois life style.

Also the targets that are chosen are new from this crop of rioters/activists. There is a pattern of destroying things that are more sensitive and long term strategic for a foreign interest to destroy. There is an overlap that suit both the low end malcontents who rage against the discipline of the wheel—that's my take— and slavery abuse activists who want more affirmative actions up to and including reparations. On top of that there could be angry foreign powers that the United States have gratuitously insulted are using the unrest for their own purposes. Kind of a schadenfreude experience.

Examples of strategic targets are those that eat away at American cohesiveness. The targets are statues that have historical significance to America. Statues of Christopher Columbus, missionaries from Europe, former presidents, paintings and statues of former Southern States, members of congress during the post Civil War era, statues of Confederate generals. Their logic is to divide and conquer. Opt for more than regime change but for different government duties and powers. Simply change America from a capitalist country to a communist country.

It would fit. Better strategy than invading a strategically superior super power like the U.S. It's easier to foment a civil war along civil rights philosophies.

Osama bin Laden didn't care about blacks when

he rammed the World Trade Center. He was getting back at the scourge of peace on earth—-the United States. He didn't like what the United States was doing in the Middle East. Like what the United States did to his own country Saudi Arabia. America has supported the Saudi autocrats who rule from the backseats of their Bentley autos ! He didn't want any part of collaborating with the country who created Israel. I don't think it's the remnants of Al Qaida that are agitating. But I would believe that China or Russia would love to see our comeuppance.

The street rioters are organized by Black Lives Matter. But suppose the group isn't confined to protecting African-Americans from police. The other more important strategic goal is to cause a revolution to replace America's capitalism with a Marxist-Leninist economic philosophy. Which is communism. Also there could be a foreign power involved. I don't know. There are so many people we have alienated. Communism—-that old moth-eaten philosophy—- is pulled out of the hope chest and woven into the Black Lives Matter quilt. I looked up the founders of Black Lives Matter. They are three black women in their mid thirties. Two are self described "queers". They would be Alicia Garza and Patrisse Cullers and the third is an immigrant from Nigeria who is Opal Tometi.

A 2015 YouTube interview of Collors documents her proclaiming that she and her co-founders are advocates of Marxism-Leninism. What's old is new again? Ironic. So the successful blitz on our society is led by three ignorant women who are winning because the opposition—-us— are more ignorant and meek than they are. But the girls have determination and they are on the move. The rest of us are trying to behave like the Civil Rights Act and the penal code say we should behave. Game plan is simple. Evoke fear and guilt from the American electorate with self proclaimed righteous urban destruction and then offer peace with legislation that changes goals away from a meritocracy to a society that is consumed with equality goals. Sound familiar? It should. The Civil Rights movement is undefeated using these street tactics since the nineteen sixties. The rioters continue to use the civil rights issues as their principal weapon. But they are joined by possible foreign state actors and Marxist-Leninists radicals. All together they are formidable. Also Hollywood funds their activity both with cash donations and sympathetic coverage in the media and motion picture propaganda below the surface of the dialogue. Hollywood freaks refuse to be civilized. Therefore they fund other uncivilized freaks so they have company.

Give the devil his due. Black Lives Matter do have a very valid point about corruption on Wall Street and accomplices in our government. Wall Street constructively steals billions through government bail outs for their crimes and no one goes to jail. Certainly no banker gets a choke hold. So lets have some claw back. They have a point.

I have a fantasy of cordoning of Manhattan. And

let the BLM'ers go after the bankers. A kind of most dangerous game adventure. But no attorneys. Just give each group manually operated weapons and see who wins. After that has been determined. Then I would lead a clean up group to humanely eliminate the winners. Both bankers and street criminals are the same. Only difference is in their methods. Get rid of both.

The Modern Monetary Theory has been ignoring economic red lights for some time. Heard of the Modern Monetary Theory? It's distinction is that deficits don't matter and fiscal discipline is cast aside. Everything we were taught now is to be ignored. Sounds like Hollywood script. The Fed spawned the Modern Monetary Theory by it's first quantitive easing after the financial meltdown in 2008. The Fed created the bubble that now has collapsed and the Fed is trying to reflate with yet another Q E. Simply. We do not have an economy in the traditional definition. We have an economy based on Federal Reserve manipulation using fiat money. Our economy is now tied to a federal reserve game of solitaire that it cheats at. The fed claims to be independent of congress. That's another way of describing the fed as outside legal jurisdiction. That's a convenience enjoyed by congress itself. The fed covers up bad congressional policies by just printing more money.

So organizations like Black Lives Matter see this fast and loose monetary policy largely benefiting Wall Street and congress who are constructively the criminal class that roost on the tall buildings in Wall Street and the Capitol buildings in Washington.. They are the condors and raptors that created financial bubbles in the first place by rampant speculation with other people money and new fiat money that belongs to who can grab it the fastest. Wall Street was enabled by congress to get into risky speculation when congress repealed Glass Steagal during the Clinton Administration and When Alan Greenspan was Federal Reserve Chairman. Repealing of Glass Steagal let banks get into the stock market speculation business—— again. The banks were barred from that enterprise after The Great Crash and Depression that followed in nineteen twenty-nine.

The BLM group have a point. I agree with them on this issue. And they have accurately identified the problem. I don't agree about their ultimate goal of a Marxist Leninists society. It's not about who were slave owners in the eighteenth century in America. BLM wants communism. That's the comeuppance tool for redistribution of wealth. The armed forces will back the government and by extension Wall Street. So for the BLM to get their revenge they will have to prevail in changing the form of society from a meritocracy to one that is communistic. New York City Mayor Bill de Blasio recently announced that a Black Lives Matter statue of their own design will be displayed prominently on Fifth Avenue. Possibly replacing significant historical figures who figured in the banking business. A small victory for BLM. But no one has done that before.

Chapter XV
Hollywood Agent Arrives

"Hey Mike". It was Bernie's voice.

I stood up, Marty was leading him.

"Bernie ... so good to see you ... it's been a while ... look great ... how do you do it?"

"Am I late? ... traffic ... I walk up to six miles a day ... that's my edge ... you're fit ... saw Scaramouch with Stewart Granger a couple of weeks ago ...two o'clock in the morning ...TCM ... the movie that gave you the fencing bug ... wasn't it?"

"You remembered ... yes it was ... still is the longest recorded fencing sequence in a motion picture ... Granger and Mel Ferrer ... how about a drink? ... flatten you out a bit".

"You bet ... should we get a bottle?" He looked at the host Marty. "Bring us a bottle of Cline Chardonnay if you have it ... O K with you Mike?"

"Fine with me ... Marty some bread and olives and nibbles also please."

Marty responded, "OK gentlemen, coming right up ... enjoy your lunch at Alioto's".

"How's Hollywood these days? ... still pushing the boundaries of subject matter and good taste?"

"Count on it Mike."

I picked it up. "There was a scene in the The Graduate where a relative of Dustin Hoffman pulls him aside at the graduation party and says simply "Plastic"... implication was advice to the graduate in what field to seek a job ... at a bar mitzvah do the relatives just say 'Hollywood'?"

" Mike ... there is so much money and power in Hollywood ... the richest man in the world Jeff Bezos of Amazon just paid nine figures to Dave Geffen for the former Jack Warner estate property ... Geffen was waiting ...Bezos said 'I want to buy' ... Geffen said sold ... who would Geffen wait for? ... richest man says I want ... it doesn't get any better ... Geffen likes money ... but I think Geffen likes power more ... any one can have money...not everyone can have power ... Geffen is a spoiled brat ... I have met him and been at parties with him there ... he's sucking all available input ... weighs it mentally ... he's so curious ... and so possessive ... brat for short but he can be charming."

"Funny ... exactly the guy I wanted your opinion on ... he's also gay if you get my meaning?"

"I got it ... gay specific interests? ... and how's that interest you?"

"I heard and read Bernie that Geffen had the ear of Obama on pushing the Affordable Health Care Act and now I think he's up to something big again with other Hollywood gays ... I suspect gene-editing a la LGBTQ+ plans ... while we are there ... Geffen probably talked to Mayor of San Francisco at the time Gavin Newsom about gay marriage also ... hear anything like that? ... why has Hollywood got so gay and queer?"

"No ... haven't heard about Geffen putting Newsom up to changing marriage laws ... but I don't go to those soirees ... good question about gay composition of Hollywood Mike ... some graduate ought to do a thesis "Why Does Hollywood Have So Many Gays ?" I deal with them every day ... I have been around long enough to remember what came before they showed up ... they have always been in Hollywood but not in this concentration and not with this power and with this notoriety ... particularly when it comes to Academy Awards Oscars ... they have packed the judges for that award ... the prevailing American culture before the nineteen sixties kept them in the closet as the saying goes ... but then came the Viet Nam War and the Civil Rights movement ... the war was a perversion of sorts that invited a contagion of perversions in the rest of the country ... and then the closet opened and the gays walked out blinking in the glare of spotlights but quickly demanded more ... the women also felt free about their bodies ... and sex does sell especially in motion picture films ... despite all the Philistines in Hollywood it is a town of relationships ... I have prospered with my relationships without being gay ... how did that happen? ... I had to work doubly hard ... I think the modern era in Hollywood was started in the sixties ... the hippies and rock bands and an explosion of diverse talent formed up without a steering mechanisms usually piloted by agents or managers at the helm to tack through the cross currents of Hollywood ... the talent was rebelling against everything ... they were mad ... I was mad ... their government broke faith with them ... over fifty thousand American died in Viet Nam ... hiding body bags...crowing about victories ... illegal bombings in Cambodia...all hidden form the public ... pentagon perverts used Agent Orange to defoliate rain forests and rice fields ... Vietnamese were slaughtered with napalm and starved without rice crops and all those hapless animals who were killed ... most of those rock groups came and went like a comet ... largely due to drugs and also most had no depth of talent or knowledge of arrangements beyond one, two or three hits ... but they made millions for their agents. ... when the acts exploded ... agents looked for other talent ... but now rich agents have more to offer ... they had developed connections with Hollywood film makers and established connections with venues which would have ready stages around the world for performances ... what good is talent if no one sees or hears you ... it's like the studios had pre Paramount

Settlement ... you have to have theaters ... the agents
had backed into the old studio system coupled with
owning venues ... lot's of money flowed ... gold rush
town ... guys like Bill Graham who was Jewish came
along and became agents for the likes of The Grateful
Dead, Janis Joplin, Otis Reading and others too many
to recall ... Graham and other agents were sharp and
greedy ... but they also were value added with choosing music to cover and musical arrangement ...they
were natural talents ... not all of them but most of
them ... the great ballads of the nineteen thirties and
forties were largely composed and written by Jews
... the Great American Song Book has a significant
Jewish-American Song Book section ... some of my
favorites were Jerome Kern and Ira Gershwin, Irving
Berlin he did his own music and lyrics, Rodgers and
Hart, George and Ira Gershwin and many others ...
the agents were very helpful and brought discipline
to young entertainers from bazaar backgrounds ...
they did earn their keep with musical advice ... they
got well paid ... in many cases they got too much of
the income ... but who can protect naiveté from clever
people every minute of the day? ... youthful simple
minded talent was no match in negotiating ... all they
wanted was to perform ... they would work for next to
nothing just to get a start ... would sign personal contracts that gave power of attorney to their agent who
turned out to own the venues and negotiate recording
contracts and the money flowed in a lopsided alloca-
tion ... agents won ... impossible scheduled national
tours wore out the young performers ... particularly

when drugs and booze and sex were available abundantly ... atmosphere was seedy ... who wants to be part of it besides the young starving artists? ...turns out the gays in Hollywood were curious like Geffen and wanted relatively free money ... they jumped in with both feet ... "so the lower strata of American culture eclipsed the heretofore dominant part of the culture ... Rodgers and Hart were replaced by Jagger and Richards".

"Why the gays Bernie?"

"My best guess is the gays ascended with a drive for inclusion via conflating their personal goals with the black civil rights push and opposition to the Viet Nam War ... it was a crack in the historical foundation of the country ... a break from normal ... from there it went to a bizarro break with historical and cultural traditional roots ... everything was questioned ... the young people didn't have the answers ... but they feigned sophistication to hide their ignorance ... gays are largely willful and spoiled ... like Geffen every day is new day ... a new kick to be had ... enter drugs.. open gay antics ... women sexual freedom on full display ... and the environmental movement ... I still don't know if the environmental movement is a solid gay core value ... I don't think so ... but it served as another offensive tactic to conflate their own personal values ... with other rebels causes ... I think the push for the health of the environment was the best thing that came out of the tectonic shifts of the sixties ... reasons to break with normal was the illegitimate

Viet Nam War ... the war was a perversion of sorts
... perversions of any sort are contagious ... that
includes sex ... that brought on cynicism and a rebel-
lious response to all heretofore ideas of cultural do's
and don'ts. 'Nature hates a vacuum.' So savvy clever
gay Jews jumped into culture shaping movies ... or
was art just following life which had moved on? ... no
matter the financial opportunities were huge.It was
easy pickings ... money rolled in ... agents edge was
they recognized it and exploited it ... in that singular
'Eureka' moment the gay agents laid claim and title
... why not? ... they were entitled to it ... enormous
wealth of gay agents enabled them to pursue their
own sexual fantasies on the big screen and importantly in politics and rest is history."

Drinks were brought to the table with some hors
d' oeuvre.

The waiter asked, "Gentlemen are you ready to
order ... or would you like some more time? There is
no rush."

"I'm ready ... how about you Bernie?"

"Yes. I'm hungry ... what are you going to have
Mike?"

"I'm having 'Veggies A La Fat Joey'."

"Does it come with anything?" asked Bernie with
a rhetorical grin.

"Bernie, it's this way ... Fat Joey was the senior

member of the Alioto family and managed the restaurant for the last forty years ... recently past away ... in his honor are 'Veggies Fat Joey' ... it has everything on the plate ... so much you can't see the plate till later ... and Fat Joey 'ate it up not in a shy way' to quote Sinatra ... may Fat Joey rest in peace."

"So we will have two of the Fat Joeys?"

I nodded in agreement.

The waiter responded, "Thank you gentlemen."

"Why no fish Mike?"

"Because they swim in water ... since we started using potable water to flush toilets we sealed our fate ... potable water will become increasingly in deficit ... TV ads promoting drugs for every conceivable ailment real or imagined bombard viewers who by definition haven't anything better to do but watch TV ... consequently all those drugs and all that flushed water end up surrounding the poor fish ... veggies avoid much of the saturated fouled water ... water isn't priced correctly ... The essence of life itself goes down toilets or washes cars... homo sapiens?

"How's fencing Mike ?"

"Never fenced better ... I'm addicted ... for me there's nothing like a big sweat to enhance skill and increase vitality and to bring a calming attitude to face the world with ... fence thoughtfully and calmly rather than mindlessly and in a rush ... I love to run them off the strip when I can ... sweating clears the mind ... more you sweat the more you have to focus to use your remaining energy which require more effort which in turn requires more sweating but that focus makes me more dangerous ... and the next day you have less tolerance for letting small things annoy ... just keep going ... what do you do for exercise Bernie? ... you look fit."

"I walk five to six miles a day ... watch my diet ... I'm careful about booze especially wine with all those calories. I sweat ... not like you sweat ... but I sweat noticeably ... one bonus is the creative thoughts that flood in while walking ... I believe the subconscious knows more than our conscious ... but the subconscious needs physical movement to thrive ... it's a classic partnership ... Greeks and Romans recognized the nucleus of health and success ...I could read a book and stimulate creative thoughts but the walking is more of a breeder reactor whereas reading is more of a fission experience ... it's the heat generated by physical movement that stimulates random thinking...the warmth opens up neurological pathways... synapse ?... it's the difference between rejuvenation and exhausting ... a little weary of mankind Mike?"

"Asking me or telling me Bernie?"

"Both! Mike"

"Gotcha. Figuratively speaking if I was born yesterday it would only take till before noon the following day to arrive at the point that I am at ... irritated about crowded conditions worldwide ... feel there is an inverse relation between the volume of people and the pleasure of their company ... honest and true fans of more people are guys like Warren Buffett and politicians who need consumers and voters and some one else to pay off the debts that companies and governments run up."

"That covers it, Mike. Just flying up here today reminds me of your inverse relationship example ... so the annoyance leads to refuge seeking ... by that pivot to seeking refuge can lead into incorrect choices to distract ... which then leads to a distraction of it's own ... which makes the original annoyance into two or three annoyances ... in the old days there was enough space to move out of the way ... that's increasingly difficult to do ... life is great if you are strong and you like yourself ... or you can move to Montana ... and avoid self examination and annoyance."

"I agree Bernie. We have pets ... two cats and a dog ... it's like a private carousel in the apartment ... cats chase each other and the the dog chases the cats ... cats run into a room ... one running after another and then come out with the cats having switched positions ... dog watches most of the time because she can't maneuver like the cats ... any pets Bernie?"

"No ... I'm single and I travel ... wouldn't be fair to animals ... maybe when I retire ... I would probably get two Siamese cats ... very smart...and entertaining ... my parents had cats ... look at these dishes ...

takes two waiters for the Fat Joey's veggies."

"Yeah, Bernie ... what's that Covid-19 goal that health officials are aiming for? ... flatten the curve?... platters are wide and the pile of rice and veggies are almost parabolic ... flattening that curve will take some doing ... could be a transfer of curves ... from the plate to our waistline? ... smells good ... any restaurants like Alioto's in Los Angeles?"

"No ... there was.. ... but they faded out ... Southern California has pursued all things new ... like the hippies movement in caricature ... never mind the taste ... It's new ... and we are being so gushingly inclusive at the same time ... and don't we look so sophisticated as the added message...quest for new sure gets old ... these past years ... I have tried California fusion cuisine ... it's blending different cultural foods on one dish ... I swear one time this restaurant offered on the menu a fusion of Japanese and Apache ... It's multiculturalism at the extreme ... one thing hasn't changed ... these progressives are greedy ... soooo greedy ... the less that's on the plate surely predicts the more on the bill. One of those inverse relationships you notice. "

"Japanese and Apache, Bernie ? ... could be an oblique reference to the holocausts of Hiroshima and Nagasaki and the genocide of the American Indians by the white man ... was the dish fried?"

"Yes." said Bernie almost having a paroxysm of laughter. "Some one ought to point out that possible connection ... don't want people losing their appetites over a bad comparison ... the PC police will be summoned and a full front page rage layout will expose you as racist and xenophobe."

"Here's to good health." Bernie raised his glass. "Nice to have stimulating non PC conversations."

"Know what you mean. Good seeing you. What do you think of Fat Joey's legacy?"

"I like it. Real food albeit a lot ... pleasant world class atmosphere and great views ... is it me or are there a lot of Joe's in this restaurant?"

"You noticed correctly ... needle is stuck on Joe ... it seems the Italians are always in a rush ... to save time they repeat names of their children ... Julia is the woman's choice name ... of course those names change if one is in the north or south of Italy.. ... best way to handle name confusion is to use first names as little as possible ... saves time."

" Where are the beautiful women Mike? "

"They are in the same place where the handsome men went."

"I get your point ..." Answered Bernie. "San Francisco was a city of well dressed women who cared about their looks ... now they mostly are fat and dress like worn out hippies ... I will never agree that women's lib was an improvement over past cultures treatment ... once femininity is gone then goes respect from men and women lose self respect for themselves ... it's another fallout from progressives push for equality ... history shows women always end up with the wealth ... men work themselves to death and the women are dating in black clothes almost immediately ... they are so anxious to get going again ... Hollywood women are always fishing ... they use their svelte body as bait ... life is short ... don't sell cheap. ... put some time into your looks ... If a women doesn't have natural looks then work on the outfit and the hair style ... beauty is about symmetry ... whatever one has ... hook it together with a common message of color and style in moderation—symmetrical ... more important than looks is smarts...bodies wither at various speeds ... but the brain and intuition can be ageless ... and keep people intrigued... be good company with spontaneity that is pleasing."

"All you say is correct ... for me it's about some ones presence Bernie ...no matter the circumstances ... can the person be in control of himself or herself ... quick wit with confidence and mannered ... that makes up for shortcomings on the physical check list. Look past the cover ... what's inside counts more."

"So true Mike ... what do you think of the market?"

"We have a bubble in stocks and bonds and world wide population ... bonds and stocks will burst simultaneously ... when? ...that's the question ... population is a slowly expanding bubble that is the cause for the bond and stock bubbles ... governments around the globe have been printing fiat money to cover up their welfare policies and support the population explosion ... In growth they trust "

"How would you play it? What should I do with my investments which are largely in the Standard And Poor 500 index?"

"Bernie they may advertise the index being comprised of five hundred stocks but approximately five stocks amount to twenty-five percent or more of the total value of the index ... that is a flag that our economy is fragmented which makes it fragile which is the reason why the Federal Reserve prints so much monopoly money ... the paper plugs the gaps of bad government policies...this will end badly ... that I know ... when ? ... that I don't know ... in the end we will barter ... that's the low cost economy ... that's why Afghanistan has lasted this long ... right now we don't have a real economy we have the Federal Reserve manipulating money supply and interest rates ... Fed is playing solitaire and they cheat ... if natural demand for debt doesn't exist then the fed turns from a seller to a buyer of debt ... when will the shoe drop? ...it will drop ... everyone knows that including the fed ... the critical question that has no answer at the moment is: 'How fast will the shoe drop' ... can it be managed? ... Who knows?"

"I have one sell signal that I have complete faith in." Said Bernie.

"And it is ...?"

"If I ever see a headline 'Prominent Goldman Sachs banker commits suicide'."

Mike followed up theatrically." And it came to pass that a Goldman broker committed suicide and all knew that the end times were nigh...".

"You got it Mike. Doesn't Goldman routinely report perfect quarters?"

" I don't think 'routinely' is the right word ... the fact that they do at all is astounding ... past years have seen Goldman Sachs report some perfect quarterly performances ... that means no losing days at all ... and some of those quarters are generating five to ten billion dollars in revenue ... no firm has ever done that feat ... that's as successful as a law firm ... they never lose either ... sounds like components of the devil ... Goldman is supposed to be in the "risk" business ... 'no losing days' phenomenon proves they lie when they describe what they do as a 'risk' business ... stealing would be more accurate ... particularly when they get hit with a perfect storm and the government bails them out immediately ... I remember when Goldman was called up to give testimony about it's role in the financial collapse in 2008 ... Goldman Sachs executives who were giving testimony to United States Senators ... Goldman execs kept referring to their clients as 'savvy investors who understood complex financial derivatives' ... oh yea? ... then everyone knew that they had the capability to bring down the whole worlds economy ... how savvy is that? ... they don't even lie well ... because they don't think they have to try ... after all they bought every one of the members of congress that are asking the questions ... remember $140 oil about twelve years ago? ... another crime committed by Wall Street that no one went to jail for ... guess who was at the center of that cabal ?"

"Goldman Sachs". Said Bernie with a tiresome inflection.

Mike said, "I wrote a piece on oil manipulation ... after the meteoric rise to one hundred and forty and back again to low forties ... was it supply/demand and an oil industry windfall or Wall Street manipulation— or both ? ... at least motorists can get a tank of gas from Exxon ... what do motorists get from suspected oil futures manipulators like Goldman Sachs? ...

Exxon Mobil's average wage of its eighty two thousand employees is one hundred and seven dollars per year ... in comparison Goldman Sachs' average wage of it's 26,000 employees was a staggering $622,000 per year ... +since 2000 Goldman Sachs and other Wall Street brokers had successfully lobbied for a liberalization of oil futures regulation ... Goldman has consistently wrote investment advisories predicting dramatically higher oil prices while simultaneously building large proprietary long positions ... at the same time Goldman and others created large pools of pension funds and investors to buy oil futures for their respective portfolios and thus take advantage of the liberating new regulations on oil futures ... net result is higher oil prices without a shortage as the reason ... and a large part of the revenue from increase in prices going to the criminals at Goldman and their investment pool accomplices... along with the governments help ...Goldman got to the Commodity Futures Trading Commission via Senator Phil Graham of Texas...Phil's wife was Wendy Graham who was the Commissioner of the CFTC... she changed the position limits so to allow a behemoth crook like Goldman to basically corner the market in oil futures for a one time crime of the century...Phil Graham is another disingenuous politician that regularly wraps himself in the flag of integrity ... well if it's a flag ... it should be hung ... get a rope. "

"Well Mike. At some point the whole Wall Street scam and the governments monopoly money will fall apart and we will barter our way through life ... and the winner will be — women ... to me It looks like nature will select women as the odds on choice to survive relatively better than men in a bartered society."

"Why ?"

"Because women are naturally better equipped for barter ... it's about cleavage ... women have cleavage in the front ... top and bottom ... and cleavage in the lower rear ... everything they need is owned by them naturally ... hands down or hands up ... it's no contest ... it's on board ... they don't have to pack anything not even clothes ... they can come as they are ... let the men figure it out how to woo the women."

"So Bernie looks like I need help with what you were saying earlier about symmetry in clothing? ... how can I dress like a stunning colorful male partridge who can thump his feet and attract women?" added with theatrical comic satire.

Bernie continued,"The women will observe and ask some questions ... direct questions about your job and income etc ... or indirect questions like Socrates prefers ... where you live ... what's your schooling ... where do you work ... they will ask questions and then go silent and then parse the mans answer ... women are tricky ... women have natural advantages body wise and being cagey ... man's best defense/offense is being content and secure in his personal abilities ... any one can pretend or honestly try to be some one else ... maybe they can do it for a day or a week ... but in the end no one can do it forever if it doesn't work ... be yourself ... take it or leave it ... be prepared to move on ... life is about saying hello and then saying good bye ... the only thing any one ever had at any time in history is the present moment—nunc ipsum... all the rest is speculation or memory which can be bad judgement or poor memory ... Mike, what do you think of Trump?

Mike answers," Trump got elected because people were tired of political correctness ... he stuffed the

Supreme Court with conservative justices but that has backfired in part ... last week the Court extended Civil Rights protection to gays and the LGBTQ+ acronym ... could have knocked me over ... his foreign policy has become a nightmare ... encouraging and supporting Israels Nazi- like behavior towards the Palestinians is shameful and reflects on us as the ultimate hypocrisy ... cutting taxes and adding deficit spending on top of that and the Feds quantitative easing spells financial doom down the road ... in sum Trump is yet another reason to shut down Washington and increase states rights ... no one should have the power our president has ... war should only be declared after a National Referendum in the affirmative ... the rest of the Federal governments responsibilities should be returned to the states ... politicians cant be trusted ... easier to watch and pressure one layer of thieves in the individual states then pay and police an additional layer of government in D.C."

"I can't finish this Mike. I can't take it on the plane with me either."

"Alioto's will forgive you ... you are not the first ... let's talk about Dave Geffen and the Hollywood gays plans for the future of our country ... the plans I think they have ... you know these guys ... are my suspicions plausible? ... have you heard anything concrete to justify my speculations? ... do you think it could be made into a book?"

"Go ahead Mike."

"My idea for my story sprung from the recent United States Supreme Court ruling to include gays and lesbians and all the other letters in the LGBTQ+ acronym protection under The Civil Rights Act Of 1964 ... there is no way the Court understands the nuances of the acronym components in relation to laws ... I don't think anyone understands the difference ... some of the acronym don't know who they are from one day to the next...and they want to have protection?

... protection from what? ... heartbreak? ... in my opinion there are no differences ... actually I think the acronym letters are different names for bisexuality ... as the the other option besides heterosexuality ... gays are parsing bisexuality with whims not with science ... we can't write laws for freckled face red heads ... you get my point ... you can't write laws to protect people from getting upset ... my own sport of fencing is impacted by this liberalization of sexual definitions ... men undergo transformative operations along with drug therapy and compete against women fencers ... performance enhancing drugs are prohibited in all sports ... yet transgender men egregiously ignore the other rules with the OK of our sports authorities in government and fence really disadvantaged women ... it seems to me they are up to something big ... my speculation in the extreme is they are aiming at a new race creation — and royalties from gene-editing patents ... and the recent inclusion into protected status through the Civil Rights Act is their ticket to ride ...

the the first notice occurred to me in 2015 ... that was
the year that a film called "The Danish Girl" was nominated for four academy awards ... the picture was
about a transgender romance ... it's not family faire ...
how many theater goers know personally transgender individuals? ... how many theater goers want to
know more about transgenders? ... so the film was put
into limited release ... but it won an Academy Award
for Best Supporting Actress ... interestingly the person who had received a recent Gender Reassignment
Surgery was nominated for an Academy Award for
Best Supporting Actor ... he didn't win ... but the
fact of his gender reassignment surgery received
more press space than his/her 'performance' ... his/
her name was Eddie Redmayne ... he was a female
... but in his/her first coming out film gets a nomination for Oscar as a man ... it struck me as a set up in
the extreme for publicly opening peoples minds to a
new race creation ... the next big flag that Hollywood
LGBTQ+ waves at me is in a movie in 2017 ... that
movie takes race creation to another level to say the
least ... the movie is "The Shape Of Water" ... the film
has the preposterous story line of woman having a
sexual affair with a man-fish ... I didn't see the film ...
I avoided it ... I don't know what the man-fish looked
like ... considering what the point the LGBers were
trying to make ... casting a handsome couple would
miss the point ... or it really makes the LGBTQ+ point
that looks or sexes or species don't really matter
because all are equal ... how sick is that?... it strikes
me now that maybe in the future birth certificates of

protected classes under the Civil Rights Act will have stamped "disadvantaged" in bold letters to make sure this person is never upset by anyone in his/hers life ... sorry if I wandered bombastically ... turns out the film received a staggering thirteen Academy Award nominations including winning Best Picture ... here again ... out of no where in the contemporary scene in America a love story involving beastiality or is ichthyology more appropriate? ... takes the Oscar ... since the sixties, Hollywood has been stair stepping down the treatment of sex in movies to the point of graphic pornography is on the ground floor and that's where we are ... with this ground/water breaking film...reveals a sub basement ... the object of their plot in my view is to put doubts into the minds of straights about what sex or love is ... if binary sex can be debated or repurposed then every institution or law becomes debatable ... it's like the 'cancel culture' movement that fills the media recently ... in the extreme it could include tampering and rearranging genes to come up with new sexes that are resistant to HIV/AIDS ... or just to have some fun in designing new people based on a frivolous whim ... gays are queer already and proud of it ... so who knows where their Mexican jumping bean brain will lurch next ... it's like children tormenting insects but the Acronym is having fun with the ... culture by zigging and then zagging through a now you see them now you don't dance ... when sex is debatable and love is debatable then everything else is controversial and up for new interpretations ... that being said then gene-editing becomes a very real alternative to living life...and if people can gene-edit predictably and patent those tweeks to the genome ... there's lots of money to be made ... the clincher for me and my suspicions was the arrest, trial and conviction of the Chinese scientist He Jiankui in December of 2019. Nicknamed 'China's Doctor Frankenstein' ... he was fined a half million dollars equivalent and sent to jail for three years ... he genetically altered and gene-edited a pair of embryos to try to make the embryos resistant to HIV ... time will tell ... the father of the embryos was HIV positive ... the mother wasn't ... the embryos were transplanted into two surrogate mothers ... and then it struck me what the grand plan was ... create a new race with patented gene-edited sequencing ... I think there is a chance that Hollywood money got to the 'Chinese Frankenstein' to do the experiment ... collecting royalties for designer races ... don't have to be a gay Jew in Hollywood to want some of that bonanza ... the next big thing never included speculation at that level ... plan a business model based on gene- edited race creation will create enormous royalties ... WASPy Bill Gates and Warren Buffett would love something like that ... they would be first round investors...Goldman would bring the IPO ... there's enormous potential for money but more than money — enormous power ... imagine loonies in Hollywood dog whistling amoral politicians about wanting the Civil Rights Act Of 1964 to include new race entries ... "The Crying Game" and "The Danish Girl" and "The Shape Of Water" were all trailers to soften up and dumb down heteros and some gays to accept a new race ... and The Civil Rights Act will be the Trojan Horse for what could be the next generations of Frankenstein-tinkered people ... the possibilities of what a designer race could become would only be limited by imagination ... if it works as planned ... suppose it doesn't work ... does the botched casualty get free health care and support for life? ... will there be any changes in what's allowable in gene editing ... in short will the government ever say no to 'victims' in civil rights issues? ... the protecting of the LGBTQ+ acronym by the Act gives them visibility and the authority to have a free hand without threat of extinction or persecution...they could raise money from investors immediately based only on the Supreme Court judgement ... no matter if gene editing works or doesn't work ... billions could be raised on the vapors ... the heavy lifting was done already ... the Supremes said it's OK with them to legally protect some one who simply declares that he is now a woman and the very next day protect the same self declared woman who now simply declares that 'she' is a man again ... this is insanity ... but how do you debate insane people?"

Bernie replied, "You don't ... Mark Twain said, 'Never argue with dimwitted people because after five minutes an observer couldn't know for sure who was the dimwit' ... I read an article recently about the New York City Health System being biased ... to remedy that accusation New York has allowed the sex-confused person the right to alter original birth certificates to

confirm to the latest whim of the individual ... this latest mutation in the civil rights movement is certainly
breaking new ground ... one needn't have had a sex-
change operation to qualify ... simple declaration
is sufficient ... the Trojan Horse for this new rule is
discrimination against those who could not afford an
operation ... advocates cite this as a monetary hurdle
that makes the New York Health System 'biased' ...
once you allow a little bit of dimwitted insanity into
the discussion or laws the dimwits win ... The question is ... who is queer? ... the poor confused-sexually
conflicted individual or the health officials who are
indulging them? ... the latter seem to be more queer
... because presumably they know what sex they are
but are willing to let others question and discard the
need for truth in the physical world ... passion and
emotion trump fact ... until it doesn' ...because the
truth is always lurking ... you can wrap it in billion
dollars worth of legal cement but it still lurks ... and
that's where all our debt comes from ... putting truth
in legal cement binding ..."

"Well put Bernie ... I don't know what they tell
young gay Jewish lads at their bar mitzvah ... but
it certainly contains more energy than a bowl of
Wheaties Breakfast Cereal ... they never stop ... like
any other quality it can be overdone ... is there a
word in Hebrew that means moderation? ... gays are
spoiled ... if one is spoiled then one is probably mean
also...rather than practice self discipline they choose
to change their environment to suit their appetites ...

and all it takes is great wealth and weak politicians ... both are at their finger tips right now."

Bernie replied, "Yes there is a word for moderation in Hebrew it's 'MADe' ra SH(e)n' ... have I heard anything about gene editing coming out of Hollywood? ... I have not ... But know of the movies you cited ... I didn't know of the Chinese Dr Frankenstein ... putting it all together it does make a circumstantial and rhetorical case for a conspiracy along the lines that you are speculating ... yes ... it will make a good book?... if it's written well ... don't preach ... stick to facts ... you can speculate on the meaning of those facts ... but that's OK ... any thing can be interesting provided the author makes the reading of the story entertaining ... personally I would want to read your book ... if you want help in editing or presenting the book to directors/producers for a further commercial development I can do that also ... one thing may stop the Hollywood gay juggernaut into new race territory ... Civil Rights protection is one thing ... but to genetically modify the human species may change the governing and legal authority ... GMO's (genetically modified organisms) are more correctly regulated by The Food And Drug Administration ... for me it's not a civil rights issue ... gene-editing could move the issue into a new jurisdiction ... but with this Supreme Court, flip a coin".

"That distinction is valid ... thanks Bernie ... I will take you up on your valuable offers."

"Sure Mike. One silver lining about the Covid-19 pandemic ... we haven't bombed any one during this time ... I conclude that as long as some one is getting killed or dying en masse more people are happy just being alive and minding their own business ... spoiled people bore easily and that's when the trouble starts."

"Makes sense ... well put ... want some desert or coffee?"

" Yeah. I could use an espresso and a calvados."

"Make that two Bernie."

The waiter arrived and cleared the table. He took the order for dessert.

"How about those expensive cars in Hollywood? ... do you see many?

"Only on Rodeo Drive or parked by sheik restaurants ... my favorite is still the 1955 Mercedes-Benz 300 SL Gull Wing ... it came in a roadster also ... I see Bugati's and Mc Clarets ... what am I to do with a million dollars plus sports car? ... would be at a business meeting and all of sudden would have to run to the window to see if my car is all right ... insurance? ... regular check-ups? ... have a friend who has a million dollar Ferrari ... he lives in Florida ... he's driving one day ... stops for a light ... car engine stops ... he couldn't get it started ... had to have towed ... is anything worth that? ... it's like driving a masterpiece painting ... who's going to wash it? ... go to a restaurant ... some jockey is going to park it ... maybe he has a friend who can fence the car ... bang zoom ... no car ... it's on its way to Taiwan ... and all this agitation so some one you don't know will be impressed when you are behind the wheel in first gear ... cant go faster than that because you would run out of highway pronto ... and all this tech in these new cars ... talk about chaos ... how many conversations I have had about friends having their cars talk back to them about the way they are driving? ... back seat drivers is a saying that's been around a hundred years ... that's easily stopped ... stop your friendship. ... now the back seat driver is in the dashboard and I can't get to that voice to strangle it ... I predict in the very near future cars will be offered in stripped down tech mode. ... and they will sell ... oh boy will they sell ... I have a Mercedes 2009 350 CLK that has no tech to speak of or for that matter to speak with ... I'm driving that car past exotic car repair shops where I see million dollars cars parked in the garage waiting for a mechanic ... the owner is checking his credit card for available credit. "

"That's funny Bernie ... I had a nineteen sixty-nine Mercedes-Benz 280 SL ... bought it new ... paid sixty-seven hundred dollars ... drove it for nine years and sold it for seventy- two hundred dollars. ... it was bright red with a removable hard top ... had a built-in soft top ... straight six that was gutless at the get-go ... but when it got going it kept going ... the faster I went the lower to the ground the car went ... perfect aerodynamics ... I got a ticket when I was doing one hundred and thirty on Highway five in Central California ... California Highway Patrolman could have arrested me and impounded the car because I was well over eighty-five ... he dropped my ticket speed to eighty-four ... whew ... I miss not having a flashy fast set of wheels like the New Mercedes GTO ... where would I drive it? ... I cant get out of first gear ... where would I park it? ... I fence in Oakland ... park it at the curb while I'm inside? ... ain't going to happen ... too many people and don't feel can trust any neighborhood ... these carjackings and bust ins ... thieves have a central well organized fencing operation ... steal almost anything get cash from the fence immediately and the fence has it on a truck heading to Mexico that evening ... got to be billions on a yearly basis ... I have a remarkable memory of that 280SL ... ten years ago maybe it was 2010, I saw the car again ... it was parked at the corner of Maple and Clay ... that's about five blocks away from the home I'm living at now and then which is Presidio and Clay ... same license plate YIE 475 ... was in perfect condition ... I sold it in 1978 and saw it again in 2010 — thirty-two years later ... isn't that something?"

"Technology multiplied by fiat money equals constant change ... or technology multiplied by fiat money squared equals chaos ... squared fiat money include the derivatives of Wall Street and credit card lines of credit ... what do you think Mike? ... constant change or chaos best describes our experience today?"

"The latter Bernie.. ... technology multiplied by fiat money squared equals chaos ... ah, the calvados and espresso ... just in time. thirsty work and stimulus at the same time."

The waiter served and asked, "Anything else for now gentlemen?"

"No thank you ... good health Bernie."

"Thanks Mike—most enjoyable day ... salute ... good conversation is the best way to navigate problematic times ... I find out how I feel about any particular subject by engaging in back and forth conversations with people ... takes two to know what you really think? ...counterintuitive surely ... yet predictable ...it's an exercise of background breeding and conditioning facing real time environment ... how do we cope? ... conversation and exposure to real time events are like a mock skirmish that prepares for real time responses when the score is kept ... so much can be done with a look or a word not said when negotiating important relationships ... tech stops a lot of that one on one interface between mans real-time existence ... tech stops human experience ... more we use tech the less we are hands on ... more we lose the fine points of connections ... more we are less smart and wise and are aware of nuance ... more than half of life is nuanced ... be careful not miss out on half of your life ... it's later than you think."

"Well said Bernie ... Oculus and other virtual reality mental masturbation gadgets are foreboding ...

'Brave New World' is here ... Zuckerberg's Facebook acquired Oculus ... it's kind of life on the cheap ... travel relationships and fantasies all delivered by a headset ... Facebook strategic planners figure that long term the per capita net worth of the billions on the planet will be around a buck and a half ... so deliver life at the quantum level and snag ten percent or fifteen cents of that net worth ... it will make a good quarter of earnings ... it's come to this ... that's where we are headed ... unless somebody like a Genghis Kahn type organizes a horde and hits the road to Rodeo Drive to test drive a Mc Claren ... 'A Buck And A Half Matters' will be the graffiti logo ... Genghis Khan together with his Mongol hoard controlled China, Asia and parts of Eastern Europe ... he was in the east what the Romans were in the West ... killed like the Romans killed ... But Romans left a culture behind including magnificent architecture ... Great Khan left carnage ... some were buried ... most rotted ... Genghis Khan led a mass of poor ... they had nothing to lose ... that was an asset ... they had nothing ... so like locusts they spread and migrated out to neighbors near and far ... they took and killed ... akin to day labor ... they didn't ask for jobs ... just took living day by day ... on the fly so to speak ... Genghis Khan was the leader of this taking/ sharing communit ... todays twenty first century mid- dle class is under a similar building pressure of need to find a living from day to day as did the Mongol hoard ... unlike the Mongols the modern day hoard use money as the medium of exchange ... that could default into a barter if someone could keep score of products for barter ... we have a platform like that already ... it's Ebay ... in the past year Intercontinental Exchange made two attempts to buy Ebay."

"Doesn't ICE own The New York Stock Exchange Mike?"

"That's right Bernie. It owns the NYSE which in turn owns or operates twelve additional stock and options exchanges ... see where they are going?"

"Yes. I think I do ... they are planning for the future which could be a bartered society or partially so ... barter is true value economic deals among individuals or corporations or countries ... ICE will straddle the monetary system and a bartered system ... smart cookies ... actually ICE is more wise than clever... look at what happened to Rome and it's architecture ... it crumbled ... the empire ended close to where Genghis Kahn began ... Mike ... it's called the gravity effect ... and all this fiat money we print now just makes our fall all the more steep ... barter now for the future worlds economy "

"Right Bernie ... a true cashless society would emerge ... freedom from large parts of government intrusion could be achieved ... unlike Genghis Kahn or the Romans there won't be any killing en masse necessarily ... just inexpensive commerce will bring a measure of peace and equilibrium ... until the acid in our collective DNA opens a new corrosion in harmony... can't get away from that ... this time around oral history will be the only lasting witness of the past

... because we live in the ephemeral age...no books ... just quantum impulses of silicon memory that requires electricity to recall ... but suppose the power grid was disrupted ... then it's up to an individuals ability to navigate by dead reckoning and not a GPS. "

"Do you think the government will go quietly when most people tell them to get lost and we aren't going to pay taxes?" Asks Bernie.

" They wont go quietly ... the real question is how fast the change takes place ... the more sudden ...more the violence.. it comes down to timing ... if the move to barter is glacial speed ... then probably fighting in the streets can be avoided ... if it all happens in six months or a year, then that could be big trouble for every one ... timing timing timing ... Like Astaire's book 'Steps in Time' ... fun to do ... fun to watch ...Genghis Kahn had the problem of too many people that he had to manage ... what's he do? ... turn the problem into a weapon ... Take his population on the road ... population is the problem today ... too many people ... more the people the more connections ... more the connections the easier it becomes to step on some ones foot ... then look out ... time to cull the herd ... need less population ... bring back open space and nature ... I figure maybe three hundred to five hundred million humans. Tops."

"Why that number Mike? we are almost eight billion now ... how do humanely eliminate seven and half billion people?"

"I will answer the second question first ... 'How do you humanely eliminate seven and one half billion people.' Same way we got to eight billion—tax code ... in the West we have been subsidizing family formation since day one of the tax code ... stop the subsidy ... maybe turn the subsidy into a pleasant penalty? ... offer a buyout of procreation rights ... one sure way to rein in population growth is to buy procreation rights ... I think that poor people around the globe would gladly turn in procreation ability for the right cash figure ... can still have sex but no children ... also have a tax on consumption not on income ... then every one pays their fair share ... question number one answer is that was roughly the population between five hundred B.C.E and five hundred C.E. which was the classic periods of east and west ... after that millennium, people became more and more redundant ... particularly in the eighteenth and nineteenth centuries with the industrial revolution and technology inventions basically replaced the inventors ... since then the goal is to combat boredom ... hello obesity ... hello pornography ... use a tool lose your place ... look closely at this covid-19 mess ... the actual numbers of deaths are less than the annual rate of deaths from HIV/AIDS ... but we have been conditioned to accept deaths from AIDS as politically correct and consequently acceptable ... we have been weened from critical thinking because of gadgets therefore we become susceptible to being indoctrinated by masters of the lie — Hollywood ... have eight billion people ... far as I'm concerned we are due for a significant culling of the herd ... our fish stocks and wildlife plummeted in the early seventies when world wide population was approximately three billion ... now we are almost eight ... feeding eight is the problem...more extinctions are coming ... some of the eight are eating mammals like bats to supplement their diets ... That's a no-no ... that's how we got AIDS, Ebola and now coronavirus ... for me eight billion people is an embarrassment."

"The laws of big numbers ... can't hide their consequences Mike ... life unfolding is like a baseball game ... what inning are we in?"

"Don't know Bernie ... probably later than sooner... because at this total the increase in population will come at an exponential rate ... very quickly ... innings should always be used to put points on the score board ... in this analogy ... points on the board will be less people humanely reduced."

"Here comes the fog Mike ... looks the same as it did thousands of years ago ... but the scenery has changed ... didn't they construct the Golden Gate Bridge in four years in the early thirties?"

"That sounds right Bernie ... I had an aunt who roller skated across the bridge on the opening day ... was a tough gal ... lived into her late nineties ... still tough in attitude in her last weeks ... didn't see doctors regularly ... didn't take prescriptions ... didn't wear glasses ... so how did we get the Federal Government's Department Of Health And Human

Services? ... it would deduce that the government needed an expensive bureaucracy to control votes and create dependent people than people really needed a Department of Health And Human Services."

"More than anything ... man needs a sense of humor." Said Bernie with conviction. "No matter the era ... humor is good for personal mental health and by extension it is good for group relationships".

" To humor ... to you Bernie."

" Thanks Mike ... boy this calvados is smooth and delicious."

"They say four-year old calvados is good but the best is fifteen years or older is the ultimate ... they say between four and fifteen are not as good ... a wee dram goes a long way for me ... there's some humor ... I'm Italian drinking French apple brandy and commenting with a Scottish phrase to a Jew. "

"Bravo Mike. I'm a Jew complementing you in Italian."

"What's the difference in describing oneself as a Jew or describing oneself as Jewish?"

Bernie looked a little puzzled yet he knew the validity of the question.

Mike went on, "In my understanding of s emantics If someone said, 'I am a Jew' that is a pure acknowledgement ... whereas if someone said, 'I am Jewish' there is a hint of reservation ... using cooking as a metaphor, in one instance Jew is the flavor while in the other application 'Jewish' is only a part of the seasoning ... am I clear?"

"Very clear. And you are correct. 'Jewish' is kind of a preemptive self conscious declaration ... for me, I am a Jew without reservation."

"While we are there, is there a difference between what a Torah Jew would describe themselves versus what a Zionist would say?"

"Zionists are thugs Mike ... in Russia they said they were Bolsheviks ... it's a non trade marked name ... Torah Jews are humble and follow the Torah ... before Israel was created Torah Jews lived peaceably through out the Middle East and Europe ... Zionists are Marxist-Leninists at the core ... they are almost autistic in their lack of savoir faire".

"Got it Bernie ... how's Israel going to turn out? ... the Likud Party is an example in the extreme of modern day Israeli politics ... their playbook is uncivilized ... former Chief Of Staff for Obama was David Axelrod ... he said after talking to Israel's Prime Minister Netanyah '...he [Netanyahu] suffers from Aspergers Syndrome...' Israel has succeeded in alienating most every one on the planet and now that include moderate Jews her in America ... which is the only country that is an apologist for Israel ... how's it going to turn out? "

"Badly." Said Bernie. "But they have over two

hundred nukes ... could be another Masada where they jumped off the heights in a mass suicide coming up ... I think Jerusalem should be an open city ... only an international honor guard should be it's security force ... ticket sales to the three major religious holy places will be the only revenue source ... explanations of the religious local and how it plays into the history of the religion will be displayed side-by-side with a secular explanation — real estate, weather and water ... with a secular and spiritual explanation side-by-side maybe there will be some mitigation of the site being exclusively holy ... or another possibility could be the population of Gaza which is approximately one point eight million people walking out of Gaza all at the same time ... I don't think the Zionists can kill that fast...something has to give ..."

Mike responds ... "King Herod was the puppet Jewish King for the Roman empire about forty C.E ... Israeli archeologists claim they unearthed his tomb some years ago ... the ironies of history never fail to astound ... what's left of the Roman Empire as represented by the U.S. has gone full circle with what's left of Herod's kingdom ... now the U.S. takes instructions from Herod's replacement ... that would be AIPAC ... Nero would be livid ... since the 1947 United Nations vote till today, Israel has been supported by American assets and money ... this has been accomplished by pro-Israel lobbies like AIPAC who effectively bribe our Congress with I think laundered U.S. foreign aid ... the Jews are remarkable people Bernie ... Assyrians burn down their first temple in seven hundred B.C.E. ... Babylonians demolish the second temple in five hundred B.C.E ... and the Romans disperse what's left in the first century C.E. ... through the intercession of the United States Palestine is partitioned and Israel is recreated ... they have climbed all the way back to where they were two thousand years ago ... and yet ... still everyone in their proximity still wants them removed from their proximity ... it's a tale of defeat and survival and now what? ... for Israel it's the best and the worst of times ... their singleminded unrelenting refusal to accept defeat is astounding ... and what can stop them? ... greed can stop them ... it would seem that no matter how they succeed they are threatened by their own greed ... overplaying their hand ... now Israel is talking about annexing parts of the West Bank ... it's tantamount to a speed up of a slow motion genocide of the Palestinians ... quest for victory at any price is also their vulnerability ... fact may be that they still don't belong there ... according to the Old Testament of the Bible ... it describes a small group of Jews who were outnumbered and moving into another domain called Philistia. Philistia is the ancient name for Palestine ... according to their own Hebrew Bible in the Book Of Isaiah.

'... they will swoop down on the backs of the Philistines (Palestinians) in the west, ... they shall plunder the people of the east ... put forth their hand against Edom and Moab ... Ammonites shall obey them. ... Lord will utterly destroy the tongue of the

MY LUNCH WITH A HOLLYWOOD AGENT

Sea Of Egypt (Dead Sea).'

Mike continued. Philistia is a Greek word for 'migrant'. Philistines/Palestinians are probably of Greek heritage ... from Crete in fifteen hundred B.C.E. ... Jews were coming out of enslavement in Egypt ... Philistines were already established ... I know possession is important in real estate law ...but how they got the land is important in criminal law."

Bernie comments, "Mike ... here's some more irony ... I read an article recently about the cost and scarcity of a wheel ... It wasn't just any wheel ... It was twelve feet tall and four feet wide and cost forty thousand dollars each ... it's fitted to those giant dump trucks that handle four hundred ton loads for open-pit mining companies.. ... the demand for natural resources has exploded with population growth and the exponential growth of consumerism ... as the price goes higher for rare earths, zinc, copper, etc the holes in the ground go lower and wider in their extraction ... have we gone as far as we can go in the evolution of the wheel with this monster wheel? ... and by implication is man's evolutionary journey and impact reaching the natural limits of our earth and will soon stagnate and/or retreat? ... so here's the irony ... who first made use of the wheel? ... archeologists found the artifacts of wheels in ancient Mesopotamia that dated back to over fifty-five hundred years ago ... Mesopotamia is in modern day Iraq ... what a coincidence ... now the descendants from the cradle of civilization are back waging war amongst each other that threatens all civilization ... what a difference from the small discreet foot prints of our ancestors over sixty thousand years ago in Africa and the the wheel print of the vehicle those descendants use today."

"We humans are traveling in circles Bernie ... but it's the trip that counts ... like our lunch today ... we made the most of our moment which is the only thing anybody ever had whoever lived ".

About The Author

Barry Leonardini studied Greek and Roman classic history at Saint Ignatius College Preparatory and then attended University Of San Francisco where he studied philosophy. He is retired from self employment in trading financial markets. He now lives in San Francisco.

CPSIA information can be obtained
at www.ICGtesting.com
Printed in the USA
FSHW020238230121
77840FS

9 781587 905568